SOURCES

SOURCES

A MEMOIR

■

UTA HAGEN

with drawings by the author

Performing Arts Journal Publications
New York City

Library of Congress Cataloging in Publication Data
Sources
Library of Congress Catalog Card No.: 82-62095
ISBN: 0-933826-54-0 (Cloth)
ISBN: 0-933826-55-9 (Paper)

Design: Gautam Dasgupta
Printed in the United States of America

Publication of this book has been made possible in part by a grant from the National Endowment for the Arts, Washington, D.C., a federal agency, and public funds received from the New York State Council on the Arts.

Thanks to Alexander Schneider for use of Saul Steinberg's drawing, and thanks to Saul Steinberg for permission to print it.

For Teresa
My Beloved Grandchild

Contents

Dedication to Teresa

While mowing grass one sunny day, above the whirring of the motor I seemed to hear my mother singing out my name. I pressed against the handle using all my weight to manage a steep slope and heard it once again. What did it mean? Then I began to burn with thoughts that you, Teresa, had a right to know what a fantastic creature she had been. The mower coasted down again and I mused on about how much I loved her still. And, as the pungent smell of the cut grass enveloped me, I marveled that her influence seemed just as potent now as when she died in 1938. I filled the cart with clippings of the grass, convinced that I should share her life with you to let you gain from her particular vision of the world. I looked back at the velvet lawn and went indoors, content that I would soon begin to tell her story.

Thyra Leisner came from the border town of Flensburg

(which was first Danish, later German by a plebiscite). Always slender, slight of height, she held her head high, tilted just a little, almost challenging. Her ash-blond hair was pulled back in a bun. To fit the times, she later cropped it short. Blue eyes could see through anything. Her mouth was arched, on rare occasions she painted it with lipstick. Some things she wore that I remember vividly: a Russian coat that fastened with silk frogs, a matching hat, a clinging evening gown of coal black satin, a silken rose which trailed across one shoulder. I can't recall her daily dresses except that they were always smooth and clean. To me she was so beautiful, no photo did her justice. When she was twenty-six, she married Oskar Hagen. He was her age and came from Wiesbaden (a spa in southern Germany) the son of a musician. He started out in music, too, but then became an art historian. Their love was passionate throughout their life. And what did mother do? She made a home, she sang, she taught, and with it all, she *gave*. She fought for freedom, independence, and responsible achievement for every individual, and so she influenced a whole community.

For many months I read her diaries, correspondence, and words that others wrote about her. I searched my memory for actions and events that would enliven her. The more I learned, the less I seemed to know. She stayed ideal with none of the apparent weaknesses or negative traits that round out human beings. I questioned if it's possible to really know a parent. We may retain a certain clarity about our mate, our children and our closest friends, but parent figures fill a certain niche of needs and expectations which preclude awareness of their personal conflicts. Perhaps if I had grown to full maturity before my mother died, I might have found the objectivity I needed to portray her.

I read through all her travel journals and discovered that they might have been my own, sensing and evaluating what she saw with eyes and mind, whether in nature or in art. I simply *loved* her. But a passionate tale about a perfect person must wear thin.

The more I searched my mind for incidents and things I'd shared with her, the more I was confronted by experiences in nature then in art, the myriad ways in which she'd opened up my mind and senses to the wonders that surrounded me. Her concepts were reflected even in the act of gardening:

"Don't smother the plant, give it freedom."

"Work with nature, don't violate it."

"Make order to allow for growth, not as an end in itself."

She allowed me undisturbed privacy, but always seemed to be there if I needed her. Now her advice seems like the mulch that keeps out weeds and holds the moisture in to feed the roots of plants. And then comparisons were drawn between the elements of nature and of art. Once having listened to the "Pastoral Symphony," you heard the birds quite differently and saw a field anew, you felt a storm or rushing river right through your being. Or, if you really looked at Dürer's violets, you were quite sure to pick them tenderly. (I think that she in turn had learned that from my father.)

She taught me more. She taught:

Breathe deeply, look hard, listen well. Touch gently. Taste all. Embrace, help, be thankful. And when you *feel*, express it.

And I'll express it now, for you my Tessa, not mother's life but mine. Perhaps your questions will be answered then.

PART I
GERMANY

The Island

I dug bare toes into a mountain of the silky sand, long blades of dune grass whipped my legs and then, I reached the summit. Below, the sight of boundless, shining liquid stunned me for a moment before I shouted, "Many water!" With open arms, embracing it, I tumbled on into the sea.

Cold darkness slapped me hard before engulfing me. Eyes, nose and mouth filled with salt wetness. I was in shock before I was pulled back and wrapped in soothing arms. It was the ocean, they explained, not an enormous bath.

A long time passed before I dared new explorations of this world. Then I edged slowly toward it, toe by toe.

It was on Sylt, an island off the coast of Schleswig Holstein; a scene of pebbly shores and jutting dunes, of moors, of heather, and a marshy, inland lake. Small villages were settled by the Fresian natives who wore clothes they wove by hand from wool of grazing sheep. The houses were of dark, red brick with tan thatched roofs. New settlers had to build in the same manner. The house of my maternal aunt was still more fanciful because it was completely round with pie-shaped rooms. My favorite one was underneath a gable. Right through the window, I could pluck the straw from the thatched roof and suck on it.

My early memories are of images and sounds, sensations, and a few events. No thinking, only feelings.

The sea with waves and tides that pulled the water in and out, the wind that whipped the waves up into pounding whorls or blowing crests of froth, were seen and smelled and strongly felt. When standing with my back to it, my naked buttocks tight with wild anticipation of a smacking wave, I was surprised each time it knocked me down, poured over me, or burst with foam to tickle flesh and make me hoot with laughter; fright or delight, but always an adventure.

Sometimes, when it was ominously green against grey skies with surface turbulance, it was quite warm. Or when the sun glared on the deep blue, even waves, it could be cold enough to numb my hands and feet. When water was most clear, I stood in it and looked down at my feet in rippling sand as they, in turn, began to wave and ripple.

A different world began right at the water's edge. I sat there, digging in my heels, arms propped behind, hands down to hold me in position. The tide brought in the water with a gush, surrounding me until the ebb-tide sucked it out again and left small gullies round and under me. I held my breath and waited for each movement of the tide. When day dreams drifted in because the rhythm grew monotonous, a larger wave doused over me to wash them out again.

A little further back, I packed down hills of sand and poked some holes in them to represent the windows of a castle. I dug a groove around the edge to catch the ocean in the moat as it moved in and out.

The damp cool sand, so ready for my castles and my drawings, could also threaten me on the occasions when a glossy sea brought up a jelly fish on shore. I screamed when globs of pulsating transparency, with fuzzy hair that billowed from their sides, were washed against me. The tentacles wrapped round my legs and burned like fire, while their gelatinous centers stuck like glue.

At times the sun burned down and blistered me until I felt as if I were seared skin with nothing underneath it. Then Mama made a snow-white paste of water and potato flour. She smoothed it on my back and chest, she covered arms and legs, my face, especially my nose. She held a mirror up to show that I resembled a Picasso clown. It cooled my flesh and soothed my pain. I would have laughed, but then the mask might crack.

I made a task of chasing rolling pebbles in the churning tide. They clacked just like a train when tumbling back and forth. The special one that caught my eye, the rose hued one among the greys and whites, was snatched up from the rest and rubbed and held and saved. And further back up on the sand, the stones that scattered out like Klee were easy to select for shape and texture. The hours passed when walking down the beach, head down, eyes darting from one pebble to the other. The best seemed always just ahead. I squatted in the sand to rest and play. I lined up pebbles to form paths, then houses with their many rooms and families. Large stones were parents, smaller ones were children or just babies.

As summers passed, I learned to hunt for amber and for moonstones. Each one seemed like a wonderland when Papa held it up against a brilliant sun. No topaz matched the honey-tone of amber, no opal shimmered like a moonstone. When I confused some broken glass washed smooth and milky by the sea for a small moonstone, I kept it like an orphan in a special box.

Another world of action and sensation existed on dry sand and in the dunes. Above the water line, each family had a "basket" for the season. The basket had a wicker hood and was so tall, adults could stand in it, erect. A small bench with deep pockets at the side for storing towels and clothes was at the back, a flapping canvas curtain drawn across the front. Like territorial animals, each family built a wall of sand around their basket to create a "yard." It was an anchor and a home for daytimes at the shore. You changed your clothes, took naps, ate lunch, took shelter there from sudden rain or glaring midday sun. Your mother would be there when you had hurt yourself or some mean child had run off with your bucket.

I sat in the dry sand and let it sift between my fingers into piles like flour. I covered myself up with bedspreads of the sand, then slowly pushed up with one foot. When my big toe appeared, I shook with giggles. I buried my big brother to his neck pretending then that I had done away with him. I walked away and dragged my heels, the squeaking sand accompanied my song.

A storm or undertow formed jutting ridges in the sand, resembling miniature cliffs. With battle cries, I jumped from them while pushing with my heels against the edge to break them down. And as the sand collapsed and crumbled under me, I shivered with the feeling: some of the world was gone, it was my fault. I dream of that today.

I toddled easily up sloping dunes or dared my way up steeper ones with grunts and groans. The dune grass clumps were solid grips for hands and feet. Once at the peak, I crowed when I surveyed my realm; the beach below, big people seeming small, the whole expanse of sea which never was the same. I shouted for acknowledgement both of myself and of my feat.

My manner of descent changed with the years. At first, I slid on my behind, my pants filled up with sand. The sand filled every crack. I even chewed on it. I spit it out while running for my praise. When I was five, I took the incline like a kangaroo and landed with my feet placed sideways, bracing back to keep from falling down. At nine, I dared a flight right down the dunes, a beach towel for a glider. If flight was reached just for a second, it was worth the thousand tries. You had to grip the corners of the giant towel and wave it back above your head to wait for gusts of wind. Then it would billow out to lift you up. It wasn't dangerous because the hands gave first to let you fall just a few feet. And if your strength held out, as you took off you kicked straight out and aimed for the soft sand right down the sloping dune. It's probably a fantasy that I flew all the way.

I couldn't cross the heath between the beach and my aunt's house without a stop, so many lovely things were to be found along the way: tiny pink bell-shaped flowers between the clumps of heather, the buttery gorse among the gray green scrub and corn flowers stippled in the lavendar hue of erica. I stepped on thistles and plucked nettles before I learned to watch for prickly things. But, gathering fruit was surely one of the great joys of life. Dark purple berries one by one, were popped into my mouth. Or I delayed until I had a handful to cram in, to feel the warm juice squirt as I bit down on the sweet pulp.

When sampling nature's products in the house, the meals seemed bathed in light; pink in the early morning, orange in late afternoon. It filtered through white curtains. French chairs, upholstered in a faded blue, surrounded the long table. A pitcher foamed with milk, thick honey filled a jug, hard rolls were smeared with Danish butter. At supper we ate cheeses, beige and yellow and the brown Norwegian Muesost on our coarse grained bread. A single fly buzzed in the room. The light grew dim, a candle glowed. I watched the flame until my eyes fell shut.

On my way home from long days at the beach, I often took a detour to an inland sea, "Das Wattenmeer." The wind seemed not to reach its shores, stretching without a ripple to the edges of the bright, green swamp. White daisies stood among the waving reeds.

My steps were slow and measured since a careless step could lead to sinking in the bog.

It was a place of stillness, the roaring ocean far away. I listened to another song of nature here. Bees buzzed to overwhelm the buttercups. Mosquitoes sang before they stung and different birds swooped overhead, then dove or simply hopped to harvest all the insects of the swamp. A dozen sheep grazed near and an occasional baa-aa enhanced the sense of peace.

I can remember no one at these shores except my mother. When I was there alone I first experienced myself at one with nature. I couldn't analyze this mystic feeling then, but now I know that I had learned for a short time that I could be alone, *not* lonely, that afterwards I felt quite free and more aware of others.

The Garden

When I was five years old, I dreamed that I was humming while I rocked back on my heels between the strawberries whose tendrils curled around my ankles. Above me in the sun, black plums were dangling between shining leaves. A scent of lilac floated on the air and I had just made up my mind to squeeze some raspberry juice when I awoke. Disoriented by darkness, I was confused by the strange space around me, the outlines of the ugly varnished chair and bureau that stood just beyond my bed. The acrid smell of sooty carpet brought me to yowling consciousness. My mother came to hold me close, explaining once again the reason why our German garden was so far away.

We were in Madison, Wisconsin, U.S.A. We'd come with papa for six months while he was serving an exchange professorship. In this apartment with its knocking radiators, I felt uprooted like a plant that had been taken from its natural habitat. The building, on a treeless, asphalt street, stood in the business section, surrounded by some offices just high enough to keep out all the light. The contrast to my house in Germany made me aware of all the things I'd temporarily lost.

Our house in Göttingen was made of yellow brick. It sat on a steep hill. The street was made of cobblestones and was named Goldgraben (the Golden Furrow). Along the curb stood rows of mountain ash with feathery leaves and clusters of red berries. It was a haven for the twittering birds. The house and garden were enclosed by a black, iron fence with a hinged gate on which to swing with tuneful creaking. The rooms were high, the windows flooded them with light. A glass enclosed veranda off the back had shelves of potted greenery and cyclamen that bloomed in coldest winter.

In my white bed, tucked underneath a feather comforter, I listened for the clop of hooves and cart wheels clanging on the cobblestones below. A crack of light between drawn curtains was the signal for permission to get up, to go into my garden.

Each day I entered Eden from the steps of the veranada at the back and started on the path that led around the garden. There was so much to dig and rake and pick. Of course my tasks were seasonal. In August my first stop was by two plum trees on the right. They probably were only eight feet tall, but in my eyes, they swirled to towering heights, their gnarled, black branches thick with foliage. To stand on tip-toes was enough to catch the tip of bottom branches, to shake them hard for fruit to fall. Sometimes I bumped against the trunk with my behind to get the same result. I put them in the sun in rows until they grew quite hot. When gently rubbed, they smelled the same as cooking in a pot. The perfect plums were gathered in my skirt and brought into the kitchen. The fruit that squished and cracked wide open as it landed on the ground was bright, wet orange in its purple skin. Though it was seasoned with a little dirt, I popped it in my mouth and swallowed it.

A few weeks later, bright green apples and some lumpy pears began to form on trees next to the plums. The cycle of development from barest branches of the wood that seems quite dead, to tiny leaves that push out from the nodes, to the emergence of the frothy blossoms which, in turn, become red, juicy apples or rough, brown-skinned pears with snowy flesh still seems mysterious to me.

Down underneath these fruit trees grew violets and lilies-of-the-valley. When earth was packed by winter's cold, I was allowed to loosen it with a small three-tined fork. The spring rains seeped down to the roots. Then lilies-of-the-valley pushed through the earth like small green domes. They grew, unfurled, first like ice cream cones, then turned into the pads that formed a mass of green. I pushed the leaves apart to find the stalks, stacked evenly with perfect bells; the perfume made me reel.

A sandbox stood beyond the fruit trees in the far right corner of the garden. It was my brother's territory. He built elaborate castles, ramparts, bridges and placed soldiers all around a moat. One of my greatest pleasures was to knock the whole thing down.

When roses bloomed across the back, I was allowed to smell them on the bush. I watched the birch tree sway behind the boxwood hedge. When the white, papery bark peeled off, I picked it and arranged it in a box.

An arbor of green vines, a bench beneath it, was in the other corner. It was my playhouse, secret nook, a place for fantasies and, on occasion, parties. There it was always cool and sunlight filtered through the leaves in lovely patterns.

The path that led back to the house was lined with tulips, snowbells, irises which, after blooming, were filled in with annuals. Behind them, all along the fence, the prickly raspberry tumbled next to gooseberry bushes. These truly were "forbidden fruit" because whenever I would try to pick them without help, the thorns drew blood. When grown-ups picked the raspberries for me, they melted, velvet on my tongue. If plentiful, I was allowed to squeeze their juice through towels and the thick liquid gushed from the balled cloth into a bowl. I opened up a store under the overhang of the veranda and stood with pride behind a bench used for a counter while selling glasses of the juice for a few pfennigs.

Gooseberries, like bubbles of transparent green with geometric veins beneath their skin, tipped by brown burrs, were lovelier than marbles. I played with them because they were too tart to eat before they were preserved for jam. Three currant bushes just beyond, turned scarlet in July. First blossoms hung in clusters on thin, drooping stems. Then they turned into pearls that grew pale pink. When fully ripe, too tart to eat, I stripped them into waiting baskets, content to wait for jam called Bar-le-Duc.

The peonies beside the house, those balls of swirling white or red or deepest pink, so tall among their bushy leaves, were mine. Their very perfume carried on the wind in June was mine. (In Germany they are called Pfingstflumen and Pfingsten means Whitsuntide, the day the Holy Ghost came down to the Apostles. Since I was born on Pfingsten, I was convinced this flower bloomed for me.)

Next to the house, far taller than the house itself, four pines brought yet another scent, especially on hot days. Along the fence in front, sprawled lilac bushes. Their lavendar cones of star-like blossoms gave off a dizzying aroma that made the passer-by stand still.

I loved the vegetables that filled the center of the garden at the back. It was my ritual to wind through all the rows from left to right, to change direction, then retrace my steps, inventing a mock maze, then to surprise myself when I came out.

Enroute, I pinched the leaves of spikey herbs and sniffed my fingers for their pungency. I peeked beneath broad leaves to see if beans were dangling down. I counted carrot tops lined up as neatly as my brother's soldiers. I squatted down to strawberry vines to hunt for the fat fruit. I was content.

At times, the soil was ashy dry and when you kicked it or the wind blew hard, dust swirled in little eddies. The leaves of vegetables drooped down and then I helped to tilt the sprinking can as Mother aimed it at the roots of thirsty plants. When sudden rains teemed down to leave large puddles, I leaped across or sloshed right through them. A worm would wiggle out of sight into the soil, its slippery end eluding all my fingers. When the rain stopped, the sun came out above the clouds shaped like fat sheep. A large cloud with a beard could be a shepherd, maybe God.

Of course I fell, I stepped on rakes, got thorns stuck in my hands and feet. But worse things happened, too.

One fine spring day while hanging on the fence in front, I hummed a tune and stretched with arabeques. A girl came down the street with a few lilacs. I asked where she had gotten them and she was quick to tell me a sad tale about her parents who were starved and desolate. She had to beg for flowers, selling them for food and clothes. I leaped down from the fence and opened up the gate and pulled her to the garden. I yanked up flowers by the roots, I ripped up tulips, iris, bulbs and all, and then with tears and running nose, I pushed them in her outstretched arms. My mother loomed from nowhere, changed from a saint to fury and gave me one great swat before retrieving all her flowers. She wished to learn the cause of my behavior. I felt no bodily pain, just shame that acts of kindness could be treated so. I felt still more betrayed when the "poor" girl confessed to being quite well off, to suffering merely from a wild imagination. My punishment was total when my mama made me look at all the flowers I'd abused and killed for nothing.

Before my father was called back to Madison to teach there permanently, we lived in Göttingen another year. The whole last summer there, no vegetables were planted and I was free to plant some seeds just where I liked, to poke the holes into the earth and cover them with soil. When the earth split with cracks to let the seedlings through, I too would tremble. Sometimes the seedlings almost drowned from overwatering, or else, they toppled, roots and all, from overzealous weeding. But some of them survived to bloom and visitors were dragged out by the hand to look and wonder.

My brother was allowed to dig a hole, a pirate's den where once the spinach grew. He carved the steps to lead down to the bottom and paved each one with stone. Because I was a "girl," he wouldn't let me in. One day, while walking backwards looking at a bird up in the sky, I tumbled in and landed with a thud down at the bottom. The breath knocked out of me, they thought I was unconscious. I was revived and smothered with so much affection, I considered trying it again.

We set out for America when all the pears were ripe. Not knowing that I wouldn't pick them here again, I didn't cry. But once, when I was twelve, we came back for a visit. I saw a small and barren, dusty yard with patches of grey weeds and scraggly grass below some sickly trees. I wept with grief and turned in rage on both my parents for having listened to my pleadings to come back, for letting me ignore their warnings.

Much later when my memories returned unscathed to let me once again hold up that garden as a measure to all others, I forgave them.

Outside the Gate

On lovely days, after a nap, my jumper buttoned up the back, my hair brushed back and fastened with a large, silk bow, I was all ready for the meadow. I held on to my nurse and went out through the gate, turned right and walked past nine tall houses to the top of Goldgraben. The meadow, sloping part way up a hill, was ringed by beech trees, birch and pine.

I stopped to look out on the sweep of grass with patches of wild flowers. My heart began to thump while I weighed plans of actions. To run or hop, to play a little hide and seek were ordinary pastimes, but exploration of the field was filled with promise.

The grass, knee high, brushed past my legs in folds of silk. I wound my way up to the nearest splash of yellow to the buttercups whose dainty petals were as shiny as shellac. I picked one carefully and brought it to my nurse to hold beneath her chin, and when a golden glow reflected there, I told her that she must like butter. The dandelions made lovely powder puffs when furry heads were brushed against a cheek. And when they went to seed, I held the milky stalk to study the round ball of tiny needles topped by spurs. I brought one to my mouth, sucked in my breath and blew the feathery darts awhirr in all directions. Caught on a breeze, they floated on before they settled gently down to earth. I hunted vainly for their landing place to see if they had taken hold for future dandelions. The golden celandine was just too fragile to survive the trip back home in my hot fist, but clover was quite hardy. These were made up of little spears, each curling to the tip. I plucked a tiny petal from the flower and put the severed end into my mouth, then, like a bee, sucked deeply for the nectar.

I sat among the crimson poppies blowing in the wind. Like crinkled tissue, they unfolded from the yellow stamen, and at the base of every petal, coal black streaks brushed part way up. I reached out to examine one more closely when something stung my thumb, then whirred away. I screamed with rage and ran for comfort to my nurse. We watched my finger swell together.

When it was very hot, the meadow seemd to shimmer and the bees buzzed just above the flowers. If I did not disturb them, I could watch them dip into the heart of gentian or wild chicory. Their thirst for honey was so fierce, they made the flowers quiver on their stalks.

The butterflies chased one another while I chased butterflies. I saw one perch atop a clover with its fragile wings that pulsed so slowly, they reminded me of mother breathing while she slept. I cupped my hands to hold the creature captive. My fingers spread, I saw and felt it flutter in a dance of death. I tried to make it fly again and then I cried and never touched another butterfly.

If someone thought that I was lost, they usually found me lying on my back in the tall grass, comparing bluebells, bachelor buttons and cornflowers against the blue of cloudless skies. I might be counting blossoms on a stalk to find the thickest one to take back home. Sometimes I wove white daisies into wreaths and wore one on my head. Or else, like Gretchen after meeting Faust, I plucked the petals one by one to see if I was loved.

The violets at the edges of the meadows weren't just lavendar, but blue, and some were snowy white. A small bouquet was fitting to bring home to mother. When she taught me the song that Mozart set to Goethe's poem "The Violet," we wept together.

Das Veilchen

Ein Veilchen auf der Wiese stand
Gebückt in sich und unbekannt,
Es war ein herzig's Veilchen.
Da kam eine junge Schäferin
Mit leichtem Schritt und munterm Sinn
Daher, daher
Die Wiese her und sang.

Ach, denkt das Veilchen, wär'ich nur
Die schönste Blume der Natur,
Ach, nur ein kleines Weilchen,
Bis mich das Liebchen abgepflückt
Und an dem Busen matt gedruckt!
Ach nur, ach nur
Ein Viertelstündchen lang!

Ach, aber ach! Das Mädchen kam
Und nicht in acht das Veilchen nam,
Ertrat das arme Veilchen.
Es sank und starb und freut sich noch:
Und sterb'ich denn, so sterb'ich doch
Durch Sie, durch Sie,
Zu ihren Füssen doch.

A violet on the meadow stood
Bowed down and quite unnoticed,
It was a charming violet.
There came a young shepherdess
With lively step and cheerful soul
Along, along,
Along the meadow and sang.
Oh, thought the violet, would that I were

The loveliest flower in all nature,
Oh, only for a little while
Till the sweet thing had picked me up
And smothered me at her bosom!
Oh only, oh only
For one wee quarter hour!

Oh, but woe! The young girl came
Quite heedless of the violet,
She trod on the poor violet.
It sank and died and yet was glad:
And if I die, then thus I die
Through her, because of her,
Right at her feet.

(Today I always think of Steinberg when I see a violet, of the sa-
tiric comment that he makes, so different from the wild, romantic Goethe.)

"A Woman and a Man as seen by a Flower" by Saul Steinberg

a woman and
as seen by a f.

My legs grew longer, so my walks did, too. On Sundays the whole family climbed the hill that rose beyond the meadow. For quite a stretch, the path wound through the woods. Light splashed through trees and tinged the earth with orange. It turned the blue ferns yellow-green. The air was moist and pungent. I dug up mosses from the spongy soil down at the base of trees to line a basket. I found small clumps of mushrooms and a toadstool now and then. The pleated gills beneath their small umbrellas collapsed if poked too hard. Then there were chestnut trees that had white blossoms in the spring and dropped their nuts in autumn. The nuts shone just like polished wood when rubbed with oily palms. I stuffed my pockets with the best and sacrificed the rest for roasting on a fire.

When straying far behind to hunt or dig, or when I ran too far ahead pursuing rabbits' tails, my name was called and ricocheted among the trees. One nippy day, I set out with a pair of new red mittens, but almost half way up the hill my mother noticed I no longer had them on. She asked what had become of them. I answered blithely, "Thrown away." When asked the reason why, I said, "I need my fingers!" And in the distance in the grass, the mittens lay like two abandoned poppies.

The woods stopped suddenly as though a gardener had decided it. The path wound up around the hill now blanketed with grass, and in the spring, with clusters of forget-me-not whose very name and petalled face and clarion blue could rouse deep sighs of tenderness.

The last long stretch was steep. We reached the summit out of breath and stood victorious, like royalty surveying our domain. Spread out below lay squares of brown, unplanted fields, blue fields of cabbage, yellow squares of wheat, green fields of spinach, all criss-crossed by country roads with walls of waving poplars. Beyond the fields, green hills rolled softly up to meet the sky. Mist settled in the vales between and floated thinly on the fields. We sat down by the path for snacks of bread smeared with goose schmalz topped by sliced cucumbers. We drank new wine and finished with an apple. On our return we saw the town below, its Gothic spires and roofs of burnt red tile or bluish slate, all glowing in the sunset. The start of the descent was made with whoops but finished with a sleepy ride on father's shoulders.

Most days, *inside* the house, the piano played, my mother sang, my father wrote his books and worked on Händel scores. *Outside*, the Händel operas were performed for the first time since Händel's death at annual festivals in Göttigen. I was allowed to sit back in a loge to watch rehearsals several times. My father was commanding as he waved his long baton for the full orchestra. My mother was a vision on the stage as Cleopatra, Rodelinde or Theophano. Her singing was so lovely, I joined in. I'm told I sang the arias just as well as when I imitated birds, before I spoke full sentences.

When I was six, I saw *Saint Joan* in a huge theatre in Berlin. I knew at once that some day I would act and from then on began to see myself in various situations in my life as though I were the center of a play. I did *not* know as yet, that the foundations for my talent and my craft were being laid by what surrounded me.

Some years ago in England as a tourist, I wandered through the colleges of Cambridge. I went right through an open gate into a garden to admire rows of vegetables and flowers. As I came to the end, I had a sense of déja vu. There, at my feet, a river flowed, so narrow one could leap right to the other side. The greenest grass grew to the rim and over the embankment so that it looked more like a small canal than a real river. Green from the shore reflected on the water, but it was clear, each pebble on the bottom visible. Fish darted off down stream and algae swayed with every movement of the water. Moss pinks peeked through the grass along the banks. But at the very moment when a duck swam by to take a ride downstream, I knew with sharp nostalgia, it was exactly like the river I had waded in, back home in Göttingen. I saw myself on the embankment splashing hands and face, or sailing paper boats downstream, recalled the winters when it froze up glassy smooth and I slid back and forth while older children skated by.

The river flowed far out into the countryside past planted fields. On afternoons in the fall, we sometimes made excursions following its banks to fields where the potatoes lay. We camped and waited until dusk when we would not be seen or caught by farmers. But then we dug a shallow pit and filled it with some coals. We scratched the earth around the edges of the plants until, as in a treasure hunt, potatoes rolled about. (I love their German name, "earth apples.") At last, when coals began to glow, we buried them in the hot ash and lolled about the fire singing roundelays. When they were done, we poked them from the coals with sticks and tossed them high from hand to hand till they had cooled. I squeezed the charred shell till it popped and scooped out fluffy meal. The moon arose reflecting on the moving stream. When night grew cold, we huddled close around the embers, telling tales that faded into drones as I began to fall asleep.

In winter, snow flew, flurried, danced and spun when whipped by wind. Or it fell softly down in starry flakes until it buried all the streets and barren gardens. And when it stopped, no cart wheels rolled, no horses clopped, no footsteps fell. I spoke in whispers, hoping I could break the spell. Then, far away, I heard a dog, its bark a hollow echo over banks of snow. I shouted with relief.

Our sled was high, two feet above the ground, and it was named "The Flying Dutchman" after Wagner's opera. It had arched runners made of wood; when waxed, it glided slickly on the snow. I trudged beside my brother pulling on the sled. When we had reached the top of Goldgraben, I climbed in front and hung on to the knee he propped up on the sled. For a fast start, he kicked off with his other leg, then brought it up to pinch me tight and down we flew across the sparkling snow. When we had reached the bottom of the hill, we sat just long enough to catch our breath, then climbed back up again.

One time the sled was used to take me to a hospital. I had a splinter in my heel, so deep they had to cut it out. The ether made me see a lot of shining wheels while voices echoed, hollow with stacatto overtones. Then I was tucked in blankets on the sled and mother pulled me back up all the streets of Göttingen.

It was quite dark. I heard her heavy breathing. At home, I was allowed to sleep in her safe bed and all her dinner guests came up to sympathize.

On advent Sundays before Christmas, it was the custom for children to carol door to door. When the sun set, we started out dressed in the coats with pockets big enough to hold the loot; anticipation soared. Pools splashed from lighted windows, but elsewhere snow was blue, etched with black shadows cast by trees that creaked with cold and loomed like giant ogres. The stars that twinkled up above just added to a sense of being small and lonely. We stopped at windows with a lighted candle placed there to lure us into song. (When I forgot the words, the older children let me la-la-la the missing ones.) A door would open and the figures, black against the light indoors, would thank us solemnly and dole out nuts and fruits or even marzipan. As we went on from house to house—because it was the custom—our song grew faint, our feet grew numb, our hands turned blue no matter how we stomped our feet or clutched our fists inside our mittens. We huddled close and forced ourselves to sing with cheer before the final window. When I came home, I sighed with joy to be inside and warm, no longer a poor beggar in the snow.

In the spring, when cherry orchards bloomed, the family went to see the sight. However, in mid-summer when the fruit was ripe, we went without parental interference. My brother and his friends set out with sturdy strides. They tolerated me. In lederhosen their bare legs seemed those of giants as they marched ahead in time to gusty songs of nature and camaraderie. By dint of running, I kept pace with them. The road was dusty but the poplars with their billowing tops provided us protection from the heat. First we stopped at the farmer's house to ask if we might pick what we could eat. Then the big boys raced on to climb the trees and reap the juicy fruit and finally, they held me high among the leaves to gather my supply. I liked to find two cherries, stems attached, to hang across my ear. The trip back home was long, but once a wagon, drawn by hefty horses, picked us up, and while the cart jogged down the furrowed road, we lay back in the scratchy hay and chewed on blades of straw.

Late summer, 1926, before our last departure from our German home, my parents stayed behind to pack up our belongings. They sent us children on vacation with my aunt. She was a famous singer so she owned a big Mercedes-Benz. I sat in back of the convertible just like a queen while people stared and wondered who was passing by in such a splendid car. In Germany the roads were called "allees" and trees that lined them stood like soldiers on parade. In autumn linden trees turned gold so, even when it rained, it seemed as if the sun was out. I leaned back in the seat and craned my neck to watch them all spin by.

One night we stayed at an old inn beside a forest. The outer walls were painted with bright hearts, a final fillip to the fairy tale surroundings. Stowed at the bottom of the table by my bed, a flowered, china chamberpot was even nicer than the puffy featherbed. The following day, we walked into the forest and I felt that Hänsel, Gretel and Red Riding Hood lurked by. The sky was hidden by the trees and underfoot, pine needles covered everything so thickly, only ferns could penetrate. We walked on springy carpets and the stillness was mysterious. My aunt sat on a stump to rest. I built a house around her, marking rooms by pushing the pine needles into slender piles. I left free spaces for the doors and made some mounds to indicate the furniture. We had a party with pine cones as cake and mimed the pouring of the tea into imaginary cups.

The Wagner operas at Bayreuth were our next stop. I shifted in my chair, my feet fell sound asleep through many tedious rehearsals. The turbulent music that droned on and on made me hate Wagner to this very day.

But, the big farm on which we stayed for the duration there more than made up for Wagner. I played among white geese that honked and waddled on webbed feet. Pink pigs ran on short legs and gave the lie to "dirty pigs." The cow with dewey eyes chomped grass in meadows where I flew a kite amidst the cow flops. I was prepared to stay forever—until the day I ate too many of the farmer's yellow plums. Then I spent night and day enthroned upon a toilet. When mother finally came to pick me up, I was content to leave.

With tears we parted from my aunt and got aboard a train for Bremerhaven. We clickety-clacked right through the German landscape. We raced through villages but stopped at stations in the larger towns. The boys that ran along the platform peddling sandwiches and fruit helped liven up the trip and when my brother aped their garbled shouts, he made us hoot with laughter.

An echo of my parents' mood on this last stage of their departure from the Fatherland, the rain began to fall in drops that trickled down and made small paths on dusty window panes. The landscape blurred, the passing trees and houses wriggled eerily. Then water whipped against the glass in gushing torrents till everything was blotted out.

The Ocean

We pushed our way through all the people milling on the dock. The crowd was sweating, smelling of anxiety. Although the great white ship that loomed out of the water was not due to leave for hours, they seemed convinced there was not time to say farewell, to board, to check their passports and belongings. I held on to my mother's hand, my doll clutched in one arm, and we proceeded up the ramp while taking care to step beyond each little ridge, spaced like a stair, to keep from sliding back. Flags flew above the ship and people waved some little ones on sticks, both German and American. The white clad sailors with their funny caps and flaming cheeks ran busily about the deck and in the corridors.

We found our cabin down below and counted all the baggage. The musty kitchen fumes escaping through air vents mixed with the smell of fish and tar and oil and salt and paint. And when I looked out of the porthole at the rising, falling land, my stomach turned. I went right back on deck.

The time for leaving neared and an occasional twosome clung in corners of the deck or near the gangplank down below, delaying their farewells. When an enormous blast belched from the stack, it signalled our departure. I jammed my hands against my ears and screamed and felt as though I might blow back on land. Last minute visitors ran down the ramp and bumped into the passengers who rushed on board. The sailors pulled up moorings and we slipped away from shore, incongruously drawn into the harbor by a tiny tug. A band struck up the anthem with a heavy oom-pa-pa amidst the shouts and wavings. And then, when we were in the deep, the tug detached itself and chugged back home to shore. But, when the band played "Muss i' denn zum Städle hinaus," the waving hands turned feeble and the shouts turned into sobs. I joined right in, unable to say why.

The engines started with a roar that made the timbers shake. It churned the greenish brine into a boiling cauldron. Seagulls swooped down for scraps of food or floated overhead. The hours passed; we still hung at the railing. We saw the setting sun turn the brick houses bloody red. At last they were too small for dolls, and tiny steeples pierced the rim of rolling hills. Then the horizon faded. Now there was only jet black water on all sides. The engine found a steady chug; vibrations of the ship became the norm.

We dressed for dinner down below because we were expected at the captain's table. (Professors rank much higher than the rich on Europeans' social ladders.) The same band that had blared on deck now played soft dinner music. The rolling of the ship increased while we were waiting to be served and I was mesmerized by shifting glass and silverware that slid first back, then forward on the tablecloth. At the first whiff of soup placed tiltingly in front of me, I turned pea green. They took me to the cabin with dispatch. I gripped the bar attached to bunks to keep from rolling out. Pail at my side, I started retching. This went right on for days (and always happened on my transatlantic crossings).

And when I got accustomed to being tossed about, I had to face the bath tub made of tin that stood all by itself in the dark room. It was much bigger than a normal tub and squatted, like a monster, on four legs. It roared and rattled as it filled with steaming, salty water. I screamed, convinced that climbing in meant drowning or that I'd turn as yellow as the water. With lots of coaxing, I got in, but stayed up on my feet while being scrubbed, and with relief saw that my skin was pink when I got out again.

There were four deck chairs in a row, reserved just for our family. When I was well enough to go outside, they settled me in mine. I pulled the blanket up around my neck. It scratched and smelled of horses. Mid-morning broth made of brown Maggi cubes was served with crackers, good for a queasy stomach. I ventured forth onto the scrubbed oak deck. The ocean, now as smooth as patent leather, invited me to take a closer look. I stuck my head between the rails and watched the water spray out from the ship as it cut through the blue.

Days stretched from dawn to dusk with vistas of the shoreless water; changing color, texture, contour every hour. After a while, there were no nooks or crannies on the boat which I had not explored. I roosted on a wooden structure at the bow to watch our swift ascent right up each wave and then the dive, the smack with which the ship descended. With out-stretched tongue, I tasted salty particles of spray. Back at the stern, I hung across the rail and saw the engines make the water boil. Escaping oil that bubbled up left trails of floating rings as far as I could see.

I climbed from deck to deck. I peered into the open hold where trunks and boxes, loosely tied, slid back and forth and bumped when the ship rolled. A visit to the captain's bridge was often times rewarded with a chance to steer the boat. I felt that I controlled our destiny for just a moment. I played with children on the lower deck in "tourist class" and didn't understand why they could not reciprocate by coming up to visit me in "cabin class."

When I grew bored with playing shuffle board or darts, I climbed into a lifeboat hung by cables high above the deck and dreamed of pirates, shipwrecks and my rescues. I really saw a school of dancing fish. One day, I was deceived by a small speck on the horizon that grew as it approached. I thought it must be Jonah's whale, but then I saw, in fact, it was a "luxury liner." It passed close by and towered at our side. The passengers, lined up like blackbirds all along the rail, waved down at us. Then they were gone, so swifly that I wondered if they had already landed.

Beginning with big puffs of wind and lowering sky, a storm approached. Excitement mounted on our ship. The sailors lashed tarpaulins to the rails to shroud the decks. The wind increased, the canvas buckled in, then bellied out again. The sky turned black and dumped the rain in slanting sheets to dance across the water. The wind became a whistling gale, the waves turned into giants, spitting foam. I labored to climb up the deck when the ship rose and stemmed back on my heels when it lurched down again. When water gushed between the lacing of the canvas and flooded all the decks, I rushed to the salon for shelter. There, sailors tied the furniture to poles, securing everything that moved, while cups and glasses smashed againt the walls and pictures teetered crazily. The passengers, who had regarded me with pity up to then because they thought they were "good sailors," soon disappeared into their cabins. And still the storm grew worse. The waves washed over the entire boat, so ducts were closed to stop the innundation of the passageways below. Then it was like a hole in hell that reeked of frightened people, rotten food, and vomit.

At last the wind abated, waves calmed down, the sky was blue, tarpaulins were removed and ducts re-opened. Then everyone came up on deck to take deep breaths and thank the Lord they had survived this battle with the elements.

Clocks were set back each day on board until my papa said that time had stopped. And he seemed right. The air was still; we seemed becalmed, suspended. Days blurred into night. But then, a sailor shouted "Land!" and there it was, America, a thin black line on the horizon. We bustled frantically to put our trunks in order. My hair was brushed, my new coat buttoned up. I held white cotton gloves. And up we went to watch with baited breath as our new land drew closer.

The scene of our departure was reversed when a small tug chugged out and tied up to our ship. Officials came aboard by way of swaying ladders and fear began to spread; not that of leaving land but that of getting on. These government officials checked all documents and passports to determine entry rights. While standing in a line to wait our turn, a lot of whispers spread of Ellis Island, of the immigrants detained for weeks, or even worse, of being herded off for deportation.

When the unpleasantness was done, we gathered, like the gulls, along the rail. The band sat up on deck and played first "Yankee Doodle" and "America," and then some old nostalgic German songs. Then "Yankee Doodle" blared again. White buildings really scraped the sky in the September sun. A colored blob down on the pier split into groups of toothpick people hopping up and down like puppets on a string.

The moment came when everyone on board decided that they recognized a loved one down below. They changed their mind and changed their place and pushed for better views. At last, true contact was confirmed with shrieks, and the confetti flew. My uncle and my aunt, whom I had never met, were pointed out. I waved as was expected. We were among the first to teeter down the gangplank into waiting arms. When I stood free of all the kissing that went on, I thought: This land stands still, America doesn't rock.

PART II
AMERICA

New Adjustments

When we got off the train at Ithaca, New York, no horse or buggy was for hire. Here *everyone* had cars. We climbed into a Nash, our bags strapped to the roof, and started up the steep hills of the city. At last we rolled up to my uncle's gabled house. He was department head of German at Cornell, and fittingly, his name was Albert Faust. When he had brought my Tante Dodda to this house as his new bride, she must have been as scared as I was now, because she left each ugly stick of furniture, each piece of bric-a-brac where it had always been, put there by uncle Albert's mother. The Fausts were childless, loving, sweet and dull. They gently warned us all day long not to touch this, sit there, or do whatever we were doing.

The old Victorian house sat on a corner lot surrounded by a vast expanse of grass called "lawn" that blurred into the neighbor's sparse and yellow grass. A prickly hedge of "bridal wreath" along cement called "sidewalk" gave it an air of nakedness. Back by the kitchen door, a patch of herbs and flowers was their "garden," whereas the larger area all around the house was termed "the yard." Large oak trees shaded tar-paved streets and a few gangling pines grew near the spooky house. When I think back today, I know it looked just like a drawing by Chas Addams.

I mounted a front porch for the first time and stopped to ride a creaking rocking chair. My uncle opened a "screen" door before he could unlock the other one to let us in. While the adults sat in the living room to catch their breath, I ran exploring all the dreary rooms. A Bechstein piano, which my aunt had brought from Europe, was the only nice thing in the house. A screened porch off the dining room had wicker furniture: A swinging glider on a metal stand invited me to take a ride. All through the house, strange nooks and some locked doors led me to speculate about the possibility of hidden bones. Framed photos stood on everything. That day was not the only time I had to look at albums stuffed with many unfamiliar faces. On the third floor, a room was ready for my brother and for me, with iron cots and tufted spreads. The pines outside the dormer windows kept out light. I was impressed by the *two* bathrooms on the upper floors and by the white, sweet-smelling soap on every sink.

In a few days, my parents left to settle our new house in Madison and left us children in the smothering care of both my aunt and uncle. I felt abandoned, but I tried courageously to face the problems of the strange environment.

A late September heat wave rolled like lava across Ithaca. My usual run slowed to a drag. The need for screens no longer puzzled me when doors and windows stayed wide open in the hope of catching a slight breeze. In spite of screens, tormenting flies got in and it took only one mosquito "zzzzzzing" round my naked flesh to keep me up all night. The day when sunlight burned too hot to go outdoors, I sat down on the swinging couch with dangling feet and arms spread limply to the side, and filled my thoughts with the cool sea at Sylt.

There wasn't much to do out in the yard except to gather pine cones or rake leaves. I tired of the kitchen garden, too, where nothing could be touched. I had already looked at flowers that were new to me, deciding I disliked all but nasturtiums and the pungent marigolds. Coarse zinnias squatted garishly in front of snapdragons that looked as if they'd bite. The hollyhocks were colored like cheap candy. A leafless sunflower drooped its heavy head and the petunias at the edge seemed graceless, without scent.

The English language gave me little trouble, so I'm told. Within two weeks, returning from a shopping trip, I ran up to my uncle yelling, "Guck', ich hab' ein neuen COAT an mit POCKETS d'rin."

A neighbor's child became my first American friend. She taught me sidewalk games. I learned I shouldn't step on cracks for fear of breaking mother's back. I hop-scotched till the water ran in rivers from my hair and down my neck. We skinned our knuckles playing jacks and jumped with ropes until we gasped for breath. When the macadam road grew soft from all the heat, my friend dug up some hunks of tar and chewed on them. I watched with fascination, sure she'd drop dead. Then she initiated me into the rites of chewing gum. I was too thrifty to throw out old wads and lined them up on tinfoil on the windowsill for future use, in order of their freshness.

It seemed that in America, the people didn't walk, they went for rides. I didn't like it much because, aside from car-sickness, I knew already then that nature whizzing by was not to be compared with being *in* it. The engine noises wouldn't let you hear the birds or rustling leaves or sounds of rushing water. Your hands touched the upholstered seat instead of earth and plants. Instead of blossoms, hay or trees, you smelled the gasoline. My legs hung from the seat instead of wading through the water or the grass.

We took excursions to a deep brown water-hole. The older children fought for turns on the high diving board. I stayed close to the bank and dunked down to my chin, but mud oozed up between my toes. I finally asked them not to take me back. Even the clear shore of Lake Cayuga wasn't nice because of algae waving at my feet.

I was enchanted when I went to Watkins Glen and started the descent down the ravine. I gaped at the spectacular cascade that roared straight down the narrow chasm spurting foam into the air. I concentrated on the puzzle of the ever-falling water gushing with such force. And at the edge of the wide basin down below, I opened up my mouth to catch the icy spray. They pulled me quickly back, drenched to the skin. I ran along the path next to the rapids in the glen until they narrowed. I joined my brother and took off my shoes so we could teeter back and forth across the rocks. We asked how stunted trees could grow right through the cracks of rocks high up in the ravine. We spread a blanket on a ledge and had our first American picnic: boiled eggs, cold meat-loaf sandwiches, ketchup and our first root beer. If mom and dad had been there, too, it would have been a perfect day.

Soon it was time to leave for Madison, to join our parents in the middle-west. My aunt made me a present of an ugly Cupie doll. I held it dutifully in hand when, with a sigh of great relief, I waved farewell to Ithaca.

Autumn

With leaves of maple, oak and elm exploding overhead like fireworks of yellow, orange, red, my mother held me in her arms and I was sure I had arrived in paradise. And driving from the station, underneath arcades of blazing leaves, I wondered if the trees had been festooned to welcome us to Madison.

Now we were home, at 1620 Adams Street. Up in the sky, above the friendly, white frame house, migrating geese flew in a V formation with honks and flapping wings. Ouside of the front door, my parents stopped to whisper as they did on Christmas eve when they were just about to let us open presents.

My father went ahead and lit the logs in a real fireplace. In every corner of the room and all along the walls stood our beloved furnishings from Göttingen. It didn't matter that the oak and large mahogany pieces seemed crowded in the smaller rooms with lower ceilings. I cried with joy and ran from room to room. I jumped on chairs, sat on settees, a couch, an ottoman and patted mama's two-tiered desk. I opened cabinets and drawers to ascertain that all the china, glass and silverware were in their proper places.

(In Germany, all our belongings had been packed into a big caboose, whose sides were painted with bright landscapes; our name and our address swirled forth in Gothic letters up above them. Then the caboose was coupled to a train and taken to a port. From there it crossed the ocean in a freighter. To fit American tracks, the wheels were changed and then it travelled on to Madison. It ended, as a tool shed, on the campus of the School of Agriculture. It's probably still there.

A seventeenth-century armoire from Bavaria, carved of black oak, topped with a ducal, royal crest, remained my favorite piece. My grandfather had taken it from Munich to Wiesbaden in the nineteenth century, and since it weighed more than an elephant, he needed lots of help. My father brought it first to Halle, then to Göttingen, then on to Madison to house his scores and manuscripts. In 1939, I asked that it be sent to me in Ossining. From there, I brought it to Manhattan. It went on loan for several years to friends on 54th Street, then to some other friends uptown. Now, as we're nearing the next century, it rests with my best friend in Westchester where all who see it marvel. If only it could talk.

As we Americanized our lives, we gradually sold the rest of our big furniture—with no regrets.)

From the large window in the living room, I looked, beyond the willow in our yard, across the street at a small forest of red summac trees, far brighter than the flames that flickered in the fire. Our yard, both front and back, was shabby then, but mother called it virgin soil for future plants and trees and shrubs.

Then best of all, my parents showed me my own room to share with nothing but my secrets. White curtains framed the window looking out up to the sky and down at a small bungalow. A roll-top desk against one wall stood underneath a hanging shelf already filled with old familiar tales and picture books.

And on the other wall, above my bed, hung a Nativity of Leonardo. The kneeling angel looked me in the eye and pointed heavenward.

We ate our supper in the kitchen and yelled to catch up on our news. When we retired that night in our new home, we left our doors ajar and called from room to room; our laughter ricocheted right down the hall.

There were some more surprises. To safeguard our acceptance here, my brother got a bicycle and I got roller skates like those of other children on the block. Adjusting to the absence of a fence around the house, and lack of secret nooks in which to play, I zoomed as freely through the streets on my new skates as though the neighborhood belonged to me. I teetered crazily before each skid or crash. Skinned knees, stained with mercurochrome and wrapped in gauze that stuck to blood, were a small price to pay for such a splendid form of transportation. I kept the skate key on a string around my neck like a religious medal. We also got a wagon called "Red Flyer." To ride downhill, we pulled the handle back and steered with it. The wagon could be used as well for carting food, supplies and toys. It soon became quite indispensable to our new life. We polished it as though it were of sterling and never left it out to rust the way other children did.

The neighbors grew accustomed to my presence in their yards when I examined all their asters and chrysanthemums. In our own garden pansies had survived the summer and the previous owners. I helped my mother dig some holes to set out crocus, tulips and the jonquil bulbs that looked like yellow onions.

A few doors down the street, a family named McKillop had a pyracantha hedge, quite thorny to the touch, but laden with red berries. It must have been this hedge that made me take their daughter, Jane, for my best friend. The boring privet that surrounded Willard's house, and Zona's house, just couldn't hold my interest.

We had arrived too late for start of the school term, but had no trouble grasping the curriculum. Much easier than our school abroad, a lot of time was spent on things like tracing oak leaves on construction paper and cutting them to paste on classroom windows.

The weather in the fall bounced back and forth between warm, summer days and nippy ones that turned the faded grass to silver in a frost. The color of the trees blurred like a Monet in an autumn haze, or stood out, etched against the sky when it was cold. The leaves fell every day until they lay like a thick blanket on the ground. On walks to school, they swished and rustled as I waded through and kicked them high to fly just like confetti. When raked into enormous piles in yards or in the gutters, they were like haystacks to be jumped in, or else I lay on top and stared through the defoliated branches at the sky. When wind combined with rain, the leaves danced through the air like red and yellow snowflakes. A few stuck to the window panes and the big piles out in the street sank soggily. When all the trees were bare, the town filled with the incense of the burning leaves. Out in the countryside, the farmers set a crackling fire to pastures and dead brush, leaving a residue of ash to fertilize the land.

In school we learned of Halloween when we began to cut out pumpkins, witches riding brooms and blobs called ghosts, and stuck them to the windows in tableaux. On the advice of friends, we drove out to a farm (in our new car named Nabob) where you could pick a pumpkin by yourself. They tumbled in the fields like orange balls, all shapes and sizes. We chose the roundest one to carve our Jack-o'-lantern. Topped with a cap of wispy straw, we placed it on the windowsill, a candle flickering through the startled eyes and crooked smile. My mother cooked the scooped out flesh and mashed it up with butter. We ate this cottony concoction *once*; the first and only time.

We children laughed a lot while dressing up in sheets and black crepe paper. While racing through the night, our costumes trailed behind or caught between our feet. And when we neared another bunch of kids, we howled and moaned like spirits from another world or screeched like evil witches. We made believe that we were scared when they yelled back at us. And as the hours lengthened, the laughter turned hysterical;

the fear was no pretense. But, what I hated most was ringing doorbells for the tricks or treats. The way the grown-ups doled out apples or cheap candy, so smugly, so benignly, filled me with the same dread I'd felt in Göttingen while Christmas caroling; I was a beggar. I shrank away from all the rest and fled back to my home.

Our house was a short distance from Lake Wingra, its lagoons and parks and an adjoining zoo. I went with Jane to ride on wooden swings or camp down by the weeping willow trees. The lily pads that floated, with their waxy flowers still blooming in the fall, seemed always out of reach when we lay down with outstretched arms on the embankment. But we amused ourselves by running back and forth across arched bridges spanning the lagoons.

Right in the center of the zoo, behind the bars of a straw-covered cage out in the open, stood Annie Elephant. She was the star attraction. We watched her wrinkled body sway from side to side. Her trunk swayed too, in rhythm. Her skinny tail flicked just off-beat from time to time. And then her trunk curled out between the bars to reach our outstretched fists so we could drop some peanuts in the velvet hole. When it turned cold, the town came out to watch her being pulled and poked into her winter quarters.

One turn around the smelly lion house was quite enough. The hungry beasts were scary when they opened up their jaws to roar. And in the monkey house, I shivered with disgust at rainbow-buttocked mandrills, especially at the one who masturbated when his eyes met mine. The polar bears reared up like giants on their legs or plunged into a rocky pool down at the bottom of their outdoor cage. I liked them till the day I heard a boy had climbed a tree whose branches reached across the cage, and, in full sight of all the visitors, had been pulled down and then dismembered by the claws of the big, raging bear. I looked the other way when passing after that, enroute to ibex scampering over rocks or the gazelles who nursed their young.

Sometimes we had a dime to buy a gas balloon. We tied it to our wrists or to the side of the Red Wagon so it would bobble up above our heads like a good friend. We cried if it escaped and flew away. It squeaked so nicely when I pinched the tight, smooth rubber. Sometimes it burst. But, if I got it safely to my room, I let it go to hang up on the ceiling. At night or in the morning, when the gas escaped, it slithered on the floor like a small, shriveled worm.

No matter where I'd wandered, whenever I forgot the time, I heard my mother's clear soprano on the air as she called, "Oooootaaaah . . ." The other children laughed and mocked her call. When I complained, my mother asked if I preferred the neighbor's raucous crows when they yelled, "Elllinawr and Hehhhlin," and then in tones an octave lower, "Buhhhhdeee!" (just like an afterthought because he was years younger than his sisters). I stopped complaining.

The stadium was also a few blocks away but in the opposite direction of the park. On weekdays when they practiced football or on Saturdays when the games were on, the shouts boomed through the neighborhood; cheers, rahs and boos came in through all the windows. On "home-coming," alumni filled the town. It was impossible to pass through Adams Street. The road was filled with cars, the sidewalks jammed with swaggering adults in raccoon coats. Small flasks of prohibition's bathtub gin, concealed at first, emerged from bulging pockets to be guzzled in the open. Then yells came from the stadium, so loudly that it was impossible to talk inside the house and even the piano, played fortissimo, was barely audible. My parents passed on their dismay to me, disdainfully comparing football fans to those of spectators in ancient Rome who gaily watched the dying gladiators.

Frost came with greater regularity. The earth turned hard and trees were starkly bare, their branches traced like spiderwebs against a blood-red sky. In school we cut out turkeys with their wattles dangling down from scrawny necks. We drew the pilgrims with tall hats and baggy pants and buckles on their shoes. I listened, rapt, to tales about their flight, and when I learned they'd landed in the year of 1620 (just like the numbers on our house), the tribulations they'd encountered in America seemed still more real to me.

As immigrants we felt the spirit of Thanksgiving more fervently than friends and neighbors who were native born. Before the actual holiday, we drove out to the country to buy preserves from farmers' wives. From hickory trees we gathered nuts, the ones that hadn't yet been hidden by the squirrels. We ran our fingers under scratchy leaves along a bog to pick red cranberries.

My mom began the custom that went on for years of asking some poor students home to share our feast. When the big day arrived, my brother and I began our chores at dawn by bringing in the logs to keep the fire going. We decorated rooms with hanging ears of corn and colored gourds. We made bouquets of reeds, dried flowers and wild bittersweet. We covered the round table in the dining room with damask and when we had arranged the matching napkins, it was my father's turn. He loved to make a "still-life" of the table. He set out sparkling crystal, silver and our Meisen porcelain.

At one o'clock the guests arrived. By now the house was filled with delicate aromas. We drank our toasts of thanks with glasses of hard cider. The candles glowed in competition with the sun still streaming through the windows. Ringed by green brussel sprouts, the bird sat on its platter. There was a puree of tan chestnuts too, and cauliflower, and finally, bowls of cranberry sauce and relishes and pickled melon rind, so new to European palates.

When there was nothing left except the carcass of the bird, we ended with an almond torte instead of pumpkin pie. We sprawled before the crackling fire, our bellies bursting, listening while survivors of the meal played chamber music. We bade farewell to our good friends and gave our thanks once more.

Summer, winter solstices, the vernal and autumnal equinox, seemed arbitrary ways of splitting up the year. I made my own four seasons. Easter ushered in the spring and summer started when my school was done, the autumn came when it re-opened and now, Thanksgiving past, the winter had begun.

Winter

I woke to find my room bathed in unearthly light. Tucked in my bed, I craned my neck to look out of the window. The pane was covered by spectacular designs: stars shone above some mountain peaks and vines cascaded over jagged cliffs. Stalactites and stalagmites glimmered strangely in their caves below. I felt like an enchanted princess in her icy palace. I tippy-toed across the room to touch the eerie vision. The inside of the glass was thick with fuzzy ice. I scratched to make a peep hole in one corner, but only when I put my mouth up close, exhaling in warm puffs, did a small circle of the ice dissolve and spread enough to peer through. Outside, no branch was stirring and the frost down on the neighbor's roof shone just like silver paper. Sharp stabs of sunlight bounced from it so when I turned to greet my mother in the door, it was quite hard to see her face because of spots that danced before my eyes. She knelt down next to me to help interpret all the pictures in the ice.

Down in the kitchen, porridge steamed. Heat from the stove was melting ice inside the window pane into small rivulets, and it was cozy. Deciding it was time to try on all the knitted things my mom had made for cold Wisconsin winters, we put on sweaters, mittens, tassled caps that could be pulled below our ears, and mufflers, wide enough to cover up the mouth. We waltzed around as in a fashion show. Then after many kisses and our thanks, we left our mother to get ready for her singing pupils. My father set out for the University, my brother and I for school. The air was still, our breath was clearly visible. When we kept silent, air puffed from our nostrils. Our steps resounded sharply on the sidewalk and twigs snapped in the cold.

All day, big plans were made for skating, in whispers during every class and when the bell rang for dismissal, we rushed down to the lake. But thin ice slivered out from shore like broken glass and met the ripples of unfrozen water. Then suddenly, the sun was gone and stinging winds sent us back home for shelter. My mother, having just returned from marketing, was standing in her stocking feet, eyes closed in ecstacy, astride a vent that radiated heat up through the floor to let the warm air blow up through her clothing. I followed suit. We groaned with pleasure.

As days grew shorter, I went off to school and home again in darkness. My path was lighted by the pools that spilled from windows and the lamps at corners of the streets. Play was confined indoors.

The snow arrived in little spurts, the flurries barely dusting streets with tiny granules, and gusts of wind blew them from place to place. Before I could stick out my tongue to catch a flake and let it melt, it was all over. But soon it snowed again, this time with steady reverence. Enormous flakes fell on my open palm like drops of lace, then quivered for a second and dissolved. It fell down, windlessly, all day and through the night, another day and night until it covered all the roofs. The snow clung to the branches, rising thicker than the branch itself. It hung on shrubs and hedges, it covered evergreens and pines till only needle tips pierced through. The sky at midday was still grey so snow seemed even whiter.

I put on my galoshes. I loved galoshes with their rubber soles, the high felt boots that closed in pleats and fastened with big metal buckles. Four pairs, lined up together in the hall, gave me a family feeling.

When the door opened, snow pushed up against it almost to my waist. It waited to be kicked, sent flying. The steps down to the walk were indiscernible. I marked them like big funnels with my legs. I waded through the snow, delayed the shoveling that would make the sidewalks passable. Then, after just a few heave-hos, I left the chore to mother and my brother. And from his study window, papa cheered us on. He stayed just long enough to watch me lie back on the snow and, with my waving arms, make "angel wings."

I scooped a million flakes into my mittened palms to make a snowball. With evil glee, I chuckled when one splattered, right on target, on my brother's back. I put a snowball on the ground and watched it grow while rolling it on snow. It left behind a widening path that zigzagged like a maze. When it was just as round as I was tall, when it refused to budge, my brother helped to roll it to the center of the yard, the bottom of a snowman. The upper torso was a smaller ball, but all available hands were used to hoist it on its base. Next we rolled out the head. The arms were balled and carved to hug the bulging belly, a bright scarf tied around the neck. The eyes and ears were made of coal, a top hat carved of cardboard, a short stick, crammed into the corner of the grinning mouth, like a cigar. While standing back to ogle our creation, I sucked contentedly on frosty snow that stuck to wooly mittens.

The sound of shovels scraping on the walks signalled a new snowfall. Not thick this time, it covered everything like talcum powder. We made a fortress and an arsenal of balls and used the warmth of our bare hands to make the dry snow stick. Then temperatures rose, the snowman sagged, the snowballs shrank. But in the night, the weather fell to zero. The snowman froze, all stiffly hunched, his grin turned to a sneer and snowballs turned to ice.

Late in the afternoon, on my way home from school, the

hard, unfriendly snow crunched snarling underfoot. The light that came from windows was a steely blue. And then it came, a hail of ice balls pitched at me, accompanied by shrieking choruses of "Atheist!" With children at my heels, I ran from all the icy bullets hitting me. They hurt me badly even through my clothes. But, when the tyrants saw the blood run down my face, they fled like cowards.

At first my mother didn't say a word. She bathed my face and rubbed my hands and feet till I was warm. She held me close and rocked me on her lap. She said that we did not "belong" because, instead of playing bridge, she sang, my father wrote his books in lieu of playing golf or joining country clubs, my brother played the violin instead of basketball and I preferred to master the piano instead of Girl Scout's knots. And worst of all, we only went to church to listen to cantatas, oratorios, to have our spirits fed by Mozart, Bach and Händel instead of the opinions of the clergy. She weighed our values in the simplest terms: if God existed would He live in the churches or the hearts of those who talked of hate, who passed on bigotry to children who, in turn, fanatically attacked whatever threatened their beliefs? If there was power above, shouldn't it reflect the kindness, love and loyalty that man was capable of and open up the mind to wonder and to learning? My brother and my father joined our musing. We talked, asked questions, answered them, then questioned once again all through our supper and long afterward. I finally felt secure. Now I felt strong enough to like the paintings and nude statues in our house, no longer forced to share embarrassment with visiting friends. It was my right to love my Bach "Inventions" and when a school friend banged out "Indian Love Call" on our Steinway, it was my right to say, "Please don't." I could ignore the jibes and challenge the opinions of my peers and even those of the society. I'd made my choice. It wasn't always easy.

(Much later, in my second year of high school, I received a pair of bright, blue corduroy slacks. I wore them with a white wool sweater and set off for school, convinced that I looked gorgeous. To my surprise, the teacher sent me to the principal who said that girls were not allowed to wear their slacks in school. I answered that I had my mom's permission. He didn't budge from his position and sent me home, announcing: "Rules are made to be obeyed." I was outraged. My mother made me weigh my options from every angle. The easy way was to conform, to do what I was told. Did I just want to show off my new slacks? I could do that at home or after school for friends. If, on the other hand, I really felt my rights were being challenged to dress according to my taste and that these rights were being squashed by arbitrary rules, I could put up a fight; she'd back me up. I must make sure that it was worth it though. I settled for the latter and returned to school armed with a letter from my parents insisting on my right to wear the clothes of my own choosing. The principal backed down. I'd won my point, but having made it, wore the slacks throughout the term in spite of all the sneers and snide remarks of classmates. I was relieved when those blue slacks no longer fit but proud that I'd stood up for my beliefs.)

To me Saint Nicholas, the Weihnachtsman, and Santa Claus were three quite different people. St. Nick came for advent, four Sundays before Christmas. On Saturday before retiring, we'd place our shoes next to the door and he'd put gifts in them if we were good. I guess we always were. On Sundays at the crack of dawn, I'd tiptoe down the corridor to claim what had been propped up in my shoe and race back to my bed to play by lamplight with the paper dolls or coloring books that he had left for me. The last days before Christmas eve were fraught with feverish anticipation. The "Weihnachtsman" had closed off the entire living room to make his preparations. When I was very small, I'd lie flat on my belly by the door and try to peer beneath while singing carols just for him. Downtown, in front of Woolworth's store, stood Santa Claus dressed in red felt with a white cotton beard. This one rang bells and held a can while stomping back and forth just to keep warm. I gave him my last pennies for the poor and when he thanked me, I felt overcome by my own sense of goodness.

We piled our sled, the Flying Dutchman, high with packages

of cookies, home-made marzipan and loaves of Christmas Stollen. We pulled it through the snow delivering these presents to our family's friends. Each house had garlands in the windows, and wreaths up on the doors. Small pine trees out in front were strung with colored lights reflecting on the snow. We came back home with flaming cheeks and holy hearts, the empty sled behind.

At last, after a restless nap, the holy eve arrived. Dressed in my finery, I waited with my brother in the hall. Our parents opened up the living room and we joined hands and stood in silence taking in the beauty of the room. Dark shadows shrouded all the corners and danced across the ceiling to the aura all around the tree. On every bough a candle flamed and tinsel hung in silver rivulets. Beneath the tree, the presents, wrapped in colored paper, stretched across the room and when the final notes of "Silent Night" were sung, we fell upon our knees to open boxes by the hour. With crayons in the pocket of my brand new pinafore, a coral necklace strung around my neck and my new doll in arm, the climax of the evening came around the dinner table. We gobbled down the goose with prune and apricot stuffing, the skin that crackled with each bite, then stuffed ourselves with vegetables and condiments. When candle stubs sent up their licking flames, we snuffed them one by one. A last look at the toys that wouldn't fit in bed, a bite of marzipan and we retired to our rooms. And to this very day, just as I fall asleep, I think: Americans have to wait till morning for their gifts while we play Bach's "Christmas Oratorio."

On New Year's eve, we ate our holiday's hash and gathered in the living room for fortune telling fun. Like witches who prepare a brew, we melted pellets of grey lead above a can of sterno. We poured it into icy water and watched it splatter out to take strange shapes which would predict each person's future. The more outlandish our interpretations were, the more our merriment grew. The candles of the tree were lighted one last time and as they burned down low, the shadows lengthened in the room, the talk became subdued. I curled up on my mother's lap and dozed while voices, like the tide, hummed in and out. They woke me just before the stroke of twelve so we could climb on chairs to jump with wild hoozahs into the coming year.

The wind in January howled through cracks of doors and windows. The temperature sank to zero or below. Trees groaned, the timbers creaked, and snow whirled blindingly. This storm was called a blizzard. Snow drifted almost to the second floor and jammed against the doors. All schools and shops were closed; the city seemed deserted. I huddled on the window sill up in my room, clutching my knees and staring out while thinking of the exiles in Siberia. We studied lessons, practiced instruments and sat around the fire telling tales until the roar of snowploughs heralded our freedom. The people shoveled their way out of drifts that lay in rippling dunes, then hollered cheerfully from house to house like the freed prisoners in Beethoven's "Fidelio."

The lakes of Madison froze hard from shore to shore and boundaries stretched with all the new activities. I stood on double-runner skates on Lake Mendota, the largest of the lakes, spellbound by all the varied motion that surrounded me. In brilliant caps and snow suits, skaters whirled in pairs like ballroom dancers, or all alone, to make their pirouettes and arabesques. Men raced with upper bodies parallel to the ice, their hands behind their backs while legs moved just like pistons. When I watched flailing hockey sticks, I moved far back from zinging pucks. Some skaters carried sails and flew like birds right out of sight. Dare-devils drove across the ice in cars and added to the annual statistics of "death by drowning" when they plunged right through.

We usually chose the smaller one, Lake Wingra, for our fun on ice. One moonlight night when it was very cold, we skaters were aghast to see a million sparks fly from the chimney of the lion house not far away. The sparks fell to the roof and thoughts that all the animals might perish in a fire, or even worse, escape to rampage through the town, were bruited about. I got hysterical before they bundled me into the car and though I saw that all the sparks were finally out, I woke with dreams of being eaten up alive.

In February, the temperature rose for a short time. Hearts sang with hope that spring was on the way. A thaw set in and day and night the water dripped from eaves, from railings and from trees. The branches bounced, relieved of snow that fell down to the ground with audible thuds. Great slabs of snow slid from the roofs and splattered down below. The snow banks in the streets shrank down and water ran through all the weaving ruts. Then, just as suddenly, the water froze where it had dripped. The sun shone through a million icicles that hung about the town.

A fine sleet fell to shroud the world in glass; each twig, each needle of a pine was separately encased. The trees were crystal overhead and puffs of wind set them atinkling. My mother shivered when the wind arose and ripped the brittle branches from their trunks. The splintered twigs that strewed our yard were the debris of wounded trees.

In March it snowed and thawed again until the days grew longer. Then, suddenly, the air smelled sweet. A robin chirped outside the kitchen window.

Spring

There, in a muddy flower bed surrounded by wet snow, a sprig of tiny blossoms, so intensely blue it seemed to vibrate, startled me. I rushed into the house and dragged my mother by the hand to the miraculous spot. It was the first bloom of the scilla bulbs we'd planted in the fall, she said, and the green spears that pushed up through the ground would open up to make a larger patch of blue.

I speculated about "spring"—things springing into being, springing up or forth, the new year's growth. I wondered why each year did not begin with spring instead of January. I savored German words for spring: "Frühjahr," "Frühling," and translated them into the "Early Year" or "Little Early Thing."

The sparrows, grackles and the jays that wintered on, now seemed to multiply. They settled on the mounds of rusty snow. The crocus opened like a tiny bowl of sun, and for a while I squatted, waiting for the other shoots to do the same. I stared but nothing moved. I'd stare at nubbins poking through the mud and yell, "What will it *be*?" The revelations always seemed to come at night.

We drove out to the lake to cut off branches that seemed dead to me, but mother said new life would come from all the swollen nodes along the stem. At home, she whacked the cut ends with a bang, then plunged them into vases of warm water and, sure enough, in a few days the house was filled with bright forsythia blossoms. The pussy-willows broke through pods. I stroked them tenderly. The clouds grew dark and dumped the rain that washed away remaining piles of snow. The gutters ran like rivers, the gardens oozed with mud. The imprint of our feet squashed every blade that tried to grow, so we kept to the walks.

And I was restless. My parents said it was spring fever. It seemed my blood was rising like the sap in trees. Brown twigs turned green and slippery to the touch. Along the brittle stalks of roses, shoots emerged like caterpillars and weeping willows foamed with lemon yellow. A scented wind swept out across the lakes, across the town, and dried the earth. A fly buzzed through the house, and it was Easter.

Each little colored egg, a symbol of fertility, was hunted out and hoarded in a basket lined with paper grass. Hard chocolate eggs, a hollow bunny, piles of jelly beans were hidden in small nests beneath the furniture. With a new book to read, we waited till our mother served the midday feast of roasted lamb, a Schaumtorte for dessert. We heard the end of the "Saint Matthew's Passion" (begun on Friday afternoon) while lolling on the floor. Sometimes the "Passion of Saint John" was played instead. I liked it even better.

(When I was young I had four different pets that came, each time, at Easter. The first, a tiny turtle, didn't stay for long. I fed it hamburger and lettuce and flies and thought it interesting. It wandered off to disappear among the vegetables. I shed no tears. Another year, I used a present of eight dollars to buy goldfish and a bowl, supplied with underwater furnishings. For a few days I watched the fish dart in and out of castles, rocks and waving ferns. I was solicitous because I'd spent the money, not because they were my friends. I filled the bowl up to the brim with new, fresh water and the following day, the fish had over-flowed together with the water. Two were still flopping on the table top, the rest were dry and dead. I flushed them down the toilet.

My next pet was a live white Easter bunny. I loved it dearly, like a child. I dressed it in my dolly's clothes. I diapered it. It even wore a bonnet. I wheeled it to the park in the doll's buggy for "fresh air." It lived down in the cellar when it rained, and dropped its pellets everywhere. On sunny days when I had other things to do, I left it munching grass outside behind a wire fence. It must have been relieved the times I wasn't near. My mother's pity for the creature grew until she gave it to a farmer, but she told *me* that it had run away, and I wept bitterly.

My favorite Easter pet was a canary, as dainty as a buttercup. Quite soon, she dropped her first unfertile egg. It landed with a splatter on the bottom of the cage. She never really sang but tweeted merrily and hopped from bar to bar. When I would put my finger in the cage, she lit on it and cocked her head and tweeted like a hiccup. For several years she kept me company, but then she caught a draft and finally succumbed. I looked at her just once, stiff on her back, her little legs up in the air, then sobbed and moaned until my papa lined a box with silk and put her gently in it. We buried her next to the peonies and marked the spot with a white stone. She was a lovely creature.

I had to wait till I grew up to get the dog I always yearned for. My parents said because of all our travelling, it wasn't fair to any animal who would depend on us. We'd be responsible for its well-being.)

When spring vacation had to end, the rain was sympathetic. Brown grass turned green, some fuzz appeared in newly seeded patches. The sun lit up the bright blue sky, the clouds blew swiftly by. Then billowing clouds turned grey and black and crashed head on. They emptied on our heads in torrents. With the same speed, the sun came out again on the wet roofs and dripping branches. Each day, each sky, each rain was different from the last.

Soon roller skates were oiled and sounds of clacking wheels were heard on every block. The bikes were checked, their saddles polished and then they, too, whirred through the neighborhood. Their metal bells brrrringed right along with all the chirping birds.

My mother brought the sapling of a birch to plant below my window since she knew it was my favorite tree.

I almost switched allegiance when I saw my first magnolia tree. And then, I claimed the dogwood for my own when I walked underneath its branches dotted with white stars, a blackened spot on every petal. But when its blossoms fell, replaced by ordinary leaves, the birch remained most beautiful, its white bark showing through the trembling leaves.

When trumpets of the daffodil flared out and white narcissus bloomed with heavy scent, the furnace stopped its rumbling. Storm windows were removed; spring cleaning started with a furor. Our labors were accompanied by chatter and loud song. We emptied out the closets and the drawers. Our coats and suits were sent off to the cleaners, the other woolens washed at home. Then everything was taken to the attic and folded up in trunks, each layer spread with moth balls. Down in the basement, we scrubbed spreads and curtains. We climbed the stairs again and took the rugs out to the line and whacked them with big beaters until no speck of dust remained to float off in the sunlight. The house was filled with smells of wax and soap, of pine-oil and ammonia. We sang some roundelays and polished windows till they were as clear as though they were wide open. Rugs were replaced and when the starched, white curtains were rehung, I clasped my hands and sighed with satisfaction.

In Göttingen grass spread at outskirts of the town, lawns were in parks around a palace or museum; a garden was for flowers and for vegetables and ornamental shrubs. But now, in Madison, we had a conference, deciding to conform to middle-western taste, to sacrifice a lot of garden space to more of the existing grass. We purchased our first mower and took our turns to try it out. The handle came up to my shoulders, but when I raised my arms and kept them stiff and shoved with all my might, the wheels moved slowly forward and the wavy blade sheared tidy paths.

We planted herbs beside the bulbs and dug small drills for sweet peas and nasturtiums. Van Gogh's calendula were seeded next; all germinated well while it was cold. We waited till the soil warmed up and crumbled in our hands before we sowed the summer annuals.

Meanwhile in school, the term was winding to a close with written tests and orals and a play that we rehearsed. When I was in the lower grades I had already seen some real, professional plays and so I didn't like the elves or butterflies or dwarfs I was supposed to be. I thought them childish. I found a different outlet for my need to act and turned myself into the star of dramas I made up for friends and classmates. I even challenged them with tears if they did not believe me. When I was in America, the kids would prod me into telling tales to satisfy their preconceptions of my life in Germany. Were teachers really strict and cruel, were people poorer, the houses cold and gloomy? I fed them with wild anecdotes of teachers lashing me, of being locked in closets, or of fainting from a lack of food in boarding school if I had disobeyed a rule of the head mistress. And, in reverse, in Germany, the kids asked, were there really cowboys, Indians, bandits riding bareback through the streets of Madison with guns and bows and arrows? Of course, I said, and quickly turned into the heroine of situations borrowed from my reading of Karl May.

This tendency of mine once almost led to tragedy. When I was twelve, my travelling parents left me for five months in the care of a nice doctor and his wife and children. They lived in Hamburg in a suburb near a wood through which I had to bike to get to school. One day, I *really* saw some gypsies standing by their beat-up car; the women in long dresses, wearing make-up, the men in cotton pants, blue shirts, strange caps. They waved as I rode by. Before I got to school, I'd thought up a good play. I even got down from my bike and rubbed my knees and face with dirt to back it up. I raced into the schoolyard, panting, glassy-eyed and speechless for a moment. When I felt that my audience of children was large enough, I gasped; the gypsies grabbed me, tried to kidnap me. Then I described exactly how they looked and added gory actions. My performance was a wild success, the kids were sympathetic. *But*, I had frightened them and so they told the teacher. He laughed in disbelief. Then I got so upset, I wept. The teacher wavered. He took me to the principal, who made me tell it all again. By now, I think that I, myself, almost believed it and as he challenged each detail I got more adamant. He took me home and there the doctor and his wife began to grill me. I felt completely cornered and, not knowing how I could back down, I got hysterical. The matter simmered down but I eventually learned the doctor had to go to court to testify that those real gypsies I'd described were innocent and that I'd been a most imaginative *liar*.

I didn't realize till I was an adult how dangerous that incident had been until I read *A High Wind in Jamaica*, a similar tale in which a child allows some pirates to be hanged rather than admit that she had lied about them. Would I have done the same?

Back in the U.S.A., in school, I joined Wisconsin High's forensic team; my branch was "declamation." I chose long speeches from Saint Joan and Byron's poem "The Prisoner of Chillon." The team toured through the state. I always lost the contest to the kids reciting long colloquial scenes in regional dialect, but losing didn't bother me. In plays I was a maid, another time a queen, and once a wicked sister. Each time, I thought I'd been miscast; a different part seemed much more suitable. The *Journal* and the *Times* wrote of my talent, but deep inside, I knew all this was amateurish. Already then, I swooned for Chekhov, Goethe, Shakespeare and Molière and when I told them so, the others laughed or thought I was "stuck up."

Outside, the days grew warmer and the classroom windows were left open. The pages of a textbook blurred. The flies droned overhead. When heady scents of lilac wafted in, I dreamed of running wild. During recess and after school, while boys played baseball, girls played volleyball. The fun with which I entered a new sport waned quickly when an angry sense of competition rose between the players. I watched amazed when losers crept away in tears or winners puffed with arrogance.

When fruit trees bloomed in the back yards, we strolled along the alleys. The houses had at least one apple, pear or plum tree each and the untidy grounds went by unseen beneath their blossoms which seemed the climax of a re-awakening world. Out in Door County, cherry orchards spread for miles, a flowering sea, and when the blossoms dropped they lay in folds of pink and white across the greening grass.

Each June when I was small, my mother wove a wreath of daisies for my head and, peony in hand, I celebrated yet another birthday. When school came to an end, I picked an iris in my yard and waved it like a flag to greet the summer.

Summer

The grass grew bushy in the month of June. When mown, the clippings soured in the noonday sun. I pulled up weeds and dug out dandelions and then I plopped down in the shade beneath the apple tree to wait for Jane McKillop.

She brought her jump rope with the wooden handles at each end and Zona came along. Jane turned one end and Zona turned the other when I jumped high across the rope each time it brushed the alley's hot cement. They took their turns. The sweat ran down our necks, and then we opened squeaking screens and headed for the kitchen.

A fan whirred on the window sill while we squeezed lemonade. Inside the tin-lined ice-box lay a piece of ice, too small to frost the pitcher, so we returned to the backyard and waited for the iceman. The rattling truck pulled to a stop. Out climbed the burly, muscled man and used his metal tongs to grip a giant cake of ice and swing it to his leather-covered shoulder. Bowed by the weight, he carried it inside. We followed dripping tracks and watched him hoist it into place inside the icebox. When he had gone, ice-pick in hand, we hacked away at the huge block. We filled the pitcher with the shavings, chewed on small chunks and wrapped up pieces in a rag to hold against our pulsing wrists. We went back to the shade to sip our lemonade.

The sun spun out a web of heat that burned through roofs and turned the wooden houses into airless furnaces. The bedrooms were impossible for sleep. We children moved to cots out on our sleepng porch. The first night there, we lay on smooth, cool sheets and felt the breeze waft through the screens. We whispered secrets back and forth and listened to the insects of the night, the barking of a dog, a radio whining in the distance. Before I slept, the moon arose encircled by a fringe of light, made more diffuse by the meshed screens. But when I woke, I found myself on the bare mattress in my room inside. And every summer after that, the first night on the porch, I walked back in my sleep, returning to the safety of familiar surroundings.

We caught the mumps; my brother first, then father, and then I. My mother moved a third cot to the porch and quarantined us there so she could tend us all together with our medecine, the drinks we sipped through tubes of glass, and ice cream for our swollen throats. We had the lumps just on one side, protruding from the ear on down the neck and underneath the jaw. Our groans let up when we improved. We noticed the nasturtiums by our beds. We read, we drew and shot small paper planes from bed to bed. The following summer, we caught chicken pox, the summer after that it was the measles. Only the order in which we caught each new disease was different. I asked my mom why she seemed so immune. She shrugged—there wasn't time, and who'd be there to tend the invalids?

Each day I woke together with the birds in the blue dawn. Still cool outside, the grass was wet with dew. A brown bird braced itself against a stone and, with its beak, pulled at a worm, one end was dangling out. The feathers ruffled as it yanked until the worm was free to be devoured.

The temperature began its steady climb and when midmorning came, it was too hot to skate, too hot to run, too hot to jump; all energies were spent on keeping cool. While sprinklers drenched the dried out lawn, we ran beneath the spray and doused ourselves. Or when torrential rains brought brief relief and rushed through dirty gutters, we donned our bathing suits and sat down in the muddy water to our waist. We followed this by soaking in a tub of clean cold water till our skin was puckered like a corpse. We doused ourselves in cool cologne and dusted talcum on our limbs and waited till the sun went down. The air began to move and arm in arm all four of us walked out beneath the elms, inhaling perfume of the evening flowers. Sometimes we drove along the lakes to let the air blow through the windows of the car to cool us off. We sipped iced tea and ate our supper of cold aspics, salads and fruit sherbets and then we tried to read and fanned ourselves and slowly went to bed.

Quite tempting from afar, Lake Wingra had a muddy bed. The slimy weeds and snake-like waterlily stems that wrapped around my feet forced me to flee to the more distant shores of Lake Mendota. I travelled down a path of trees correctly called "The Willows" that led up to a sandy beach with clear, clean water.

I learned to float, to paddle like a dog and tread in place, my head above the water. I swam on top and under water, too. My eyes were always red, my ears were clogged, my nose and throat were red, and I was dubbed "The Frog."

This beach became the place to go. A pier was built, a slide installed for games out in the water. I climbed the ladder, sat on top, slid down the chute with a loud shriek, a smack, a splash into the water. I sputtered, spit and laughed, and climbed right up again.

I stood aside in water to my waist to watch while other children took their turn. A boy stood at the top. He crowed like Chanticleer. All eyes turned up to see. The sun reflected from the wet tin chute in rays like lightning. Then he stepped out to slide down upright, on his feet. His feet shot out. He plunged into the water with a thud. His head had struck the metal edge down at the bottom.

One woman screamed. The water seemd so black. A pool of bubbling blood came to the surface and the mother, keening loudly, waded to the spot. She pulled him up against her blubbery bosom and rubbed her hand across the gaping wound as if to staunch the flow. Thick blood oozed through her fingers until she was as red as he. The life guard pulled him to the shore. Against the greyness of his skin, the blood seemed redder still.

An ambulance wailed down the willow path. The swimmers stopped to watch him placed inside. I sat down on the sand and held my knees. I rocked myself and shivered fearfully until my mother came to bring me home. We talked for days to rid me of the nightmare.

One day I bought some crayons at the ten-cent store and walked back home by way of the State Capitol. Down a few steps ahead of me, I saw three boys. I stood stock still and stared intensely at the one who had short stubble on his head, a jagged scar with stitch marks showing at the base. I ran straight home to tell my mother: the boy was still alive, the boy had laughed!

The picnics in the countryside, with ants and poison ivy among the scrub on sandstone hills or dusty fields, were usually ugly. (Even today, I can't forget the cultivated "wilderness" of Germany whenever I attempt to plow through brambles and unfriendly underbrush in the United States with so few walking paths.) But Picnic Point, a long peninsula into the lake, was nice, and Devil's Lake, as it was called, held mystery for me. I was convinced that imps and cacodemons hid behind each jutting boulder and that crevices and cracks were passages to hell and that the deep black lake was cursed.

The wilderness surrounding it was known to swarm with copperheads and rattlesnakes, so we were told to carry sticks. We were to throw them at a snake so that the snake would strike out at the stick and leave us time to run in opposite directions. I never saw a single one, but once I heard a rattle in the brush and my imagination went to work. For weeks I told fantastic tales of an attack and how I'd vanquished the long, slippery reptile.

There was one tale I never told although it really happened: One pleasant day when Jane and I had packed for camping by the quarry near the lake, we trudged along the shore beneath the trees pulling the wagon full of gear. We came upon an old tin Lizzie by a bush, its door ajar. A man inside called out for us to stop. Jane marched right on and took the wagon with her. I was intrigued and stepped up to the car. The man was dressed quite properly. His face was red, he sat, legs spread on a grey terry towel, his pants undone, one hand around his penis. He asked if I would like to watch him "make some milk." I nodded, yes, and stood obediently by till he had done as he had promised. Then he sank back against the seat exhausted, just like the mandrill in the zoo. I thanked him very much and ran to Jane to tell her what I'd seen, in whispers. I made her swear to keep it all a se-cret, which she did, since she was sure that I was lying.

On my tenth birthday, I received a bicycle, all my own. It had been purchased second-hand, but freshly painted kelly green with polished spokes and handlebars, it glittered just like new. I swore an oath to ride on walks and stay out of the road. I pedal-led off, puffed up with pride of ownership. No sooner was I out of sight than devils tempted me to jump the curb out to the road, to tilt from side to side in figure-eights and wild U-turns. With evergrowing confidence, I put my feet up on the handlebars, my arms out at my sides and, singing loudly, raced downhill against a whistling wind. I turned a corner, tipped too far and flew beneath a backing car. I screamed and sobbed: my bike was bent, my mom would die, my pop would faint. The driver looked with horror at my upper thigh, already badly swollen, and started for a doctor. I bawled, "No, no!" He said he'd drive me home. I shrieked, "Oh, no, oh no!" Then he gave in. Pushing the broken bike, I hobbled home and told the noblest tale of all: while riding on a *walk*, a toddler ran across my path. To save the *child*, I veered into an *elm* and banged my leg and broke my bike. I never knew what they believed, just that my birthday party was still on. I limped about, my leg as purple as balloons that bobbled overhead, content with ice cream, presents and the promise that my bike would be repaired.

I waited for my puberty with reverence, for the miraculous time when, as my mother had explained, an egg would drop down from an ovary to my expectant womb and I would be a woman. The moment came. I revelled in the feeling of respect with which my family treated me. When girls at school talked of menstruation in the john as though it were a dirty joke, a curse indeed, I looked on them with sheer disdain and pity.

One Sunday afternoon, we picnicked in the woods. My father's young assistant and his wife came too, and had in tow a lonely old professor. His eyebrows bristled white. He wore a moustache on his upper lip and smiled a lot at me.

I dunked my feet into the brook and watched some guppies hatch before I joined the group around the barbecue. The wine cooled in the brook. With prohibition at an end, it flowed abundantly to wash down meat and cheese and fruit. The conversation livened up, the faces flushed and then the sun began to set. The hamper was repacked. I begged a ride in the assistant's open car and off we went, the old professor at my side on the back seat. He talked with the young couple in the front while I watched clouds that floated like a flock of sheep, their underbellies dark, their backs deep pink from sinking light. Treetops clicked by as evenly as if by metronome.

The old professor took my hand and squeezed it like a father and all at once, preceded by some mumbled words, he took my chin and pressed his liquored lips against my mouth and pressed his swollen tongue inside. His moustache stung my face. I cringed with shame and felt it was my fault and was relieved the two in front saw nothing. My feeling of revulsion went unnoticed when they dropped me off, and they were gone. I waited for my parents in the dusk and vowed I'd keep it all a secret. But when my mother saw my face, she asked at once what the old fool had done. When I confessed, she ran as though she were on fire to the phone, confronting him with passionate rage till, drained, the fire out, she took me in her arms and stroked my frightened face.

A few days later, I went out on my first date. The boy was David Bradley—a scholar and an athlete too. I was so glad he found me worthy to climb orchard trees with him. I wore my gym suit, lipstick and perfume and off we went. He praised my skill as I showed off for him. We climbed up trees or chinned ourselves and swung from branch to branch. We hung down by our knees and clasped each others hands like Jane and Tarzan. We went out to the lake where willows leaned across the water. Their branches arched so we could almost walk on them. We settled side by side out on a limb to talk about the moon that shone on us. The water rippled down below our sneakered feet. And then, the moment came. He took my hand. I hoped he wouldn't feel my sweaty palm. His head came close. Our lips met gently as we kissed; they squeaked quite long and loud. He took me home and when I walked, enchanted, through the door, my mother asked at once if we had kissed. "Oh, yes," I sighed, and softly she sighed too, "Thank God."

Except for high spots such as this, or going out on double dates to dance and then to "neck," secluded in a car or in a park, vacation days stretched on like an eternity of Saturdays. My pop was teaching summer school, my mother taught at home. I felt my days had no routine or purpose. The games wore thin, my playmates bored me, too. I stretched out hours of practicing the piano from two to three. I took a course in arts and crafts and filled the house with baskets that I wove. I daub-ed with paint and kneaded clay. I tooled in leather, pounded pewter plates. None were just right, but mother loved them all, so for awhile at least, I felt I'd worked. I played "professor" too by teaching neighbor's children "art" and other things I'd learned. And yet, somehow I knew these fields of creativity were not my forte. When mother bade me take some modern dance (she'd been a Laban and a Dalcroze pupil) I finally felt real satis-faction and progressed from year to year. I even think that for a time I wavered between dance and theatre in choosing a career.

As I grew up, I started reading all the plays my parents put before me. They got more difficult with each succeeding summer. I didn't fully grasp the problems that confronted Rosalind, Juliet or Nora, Hedda or Miss Julie, but still I worked on them with fascination. I learned the part of the young girl in Goethe's *Stella* and spoke her tragic monologue in German for anyone who cared to listen and to watch, when at the end, I swooned and fell.

I got a make-up box and studied the techniques in the accompanying manual. My diary's filled with my description of attempts to look Chinese or like an ancient crone.

My brother acted in the summers, too, and somehow, when I'd turned fifteen, he convinced the other actors at the University to let me play his sister in *Hay Fever*. I'm not so sure what Noel Coward would have said, but with the local people there, we had a great success. It was a big step up the ladder from my high school plays. The stage itself was quite a contrast to the narrow platform in the high school auditorium where I'd played or to the gym that smelled of sweating feet. In Bascom Hall I started to believe, perhaps I was an actress.

Mid-August, summer school came to an end and pop was free to take a short vacation. Three times we went to Europe for his half-sabattical, but usually it was only to the north woods of Wisconsin. They had a thousand lakes that bristled with resorts and cabins. Each time we picked a different spot: Rice Lake, Trout Lake or Connor's Lodge. We swam and rowed and tried to fish. We played some tennis, paddled a canoe. I kneeled the way the Indians do in crafts that shot across the lake. I dipped my paddle in from side to side and pushed through swamps. And when I tipped too far, I fell right in.

Some nights it grew so cold that blankets weren't enough. My father, bundled to his chin, read by the kerosene lamp that filled the cabin with an acrid stench.

On one vacation, we tried camping out, right up the shores of blue Lake Michigan. It was so huge it seemed to be a sea with sandy beaches, rolling dunes and cooling winds. But memories remain of tents that fell down on our heads and fires that wouldn't light, of pots and plates that never seemed quite clean without hot, soapy water. We seemed to be unpacking and then packing all the time until we knew that "roughing it" was not our style. Log cabin life was just about as far as we could go in emulation of the pioneers.

In the north woods, I learned to ride a horse. I rode with many others, single file along the trails. No matter what I signalled with the reins, my horse did just the same as the one up ahead. The trail went over hills and narrowed in the woods where branches brushed my hair. My gaze stayed fixed upon my horse's mane and sweaty neck and on the waddling rump of the big horse in front that raised its tail to drop some steaming apples at each turn. On the last stretch, when the whole herd began to gallop home, I held on to the saddle's knob to keep from falling off.

The summers passed and I became proficient in the saddle. I mastered all five gaits. They asked if I would lead off the parade at an important horse show in the stock pavilion. Dressed in white jodphurs and silk shirt, a jet black tam to match my leather boots, I rode with arrogance. I fell from grace when someone called from the vast audience, "Who's up in front—a wart on a pickle?" My tears welled up, but with my shoulders back, I didn't miss a trick and finished off in style.

As time went by, all horses frightened me. I felt that they were right to challenge those who tried to master them, that they should just run free. The urge to run alone came on me too, when I was seventeen.

I'd tasted freedom for four months the previous fall when papa, doing his research in London, left me alone to study acting at the Royal Academy. It didn't matter that the training wasn't great. I learned much more by living like a "cosmopolitan," by being on my own for breakfast, lunch and sometimes dinner, by going to the theatre, to concerts and ballets. I was delirious, so certain that I had "grown up." In February we returned to the confines of Madison. At the insistence of my learned pop, I entered college. Throughout my one and only ·

term I chafed, rebelling bitterly that I could find no correlation between math, biology and my predestined work in theatre. I wrote a letter to Le Gallienne and asked if one day she would watch my work to see if I was worthy of her company, to be in Shaw and Shakespeare, all the plays I loved so much. To everyone's amazement, she wrote back and said the next time I was in the east, I should audition for her; my letter had persuaded her that I was not another stage-struck kid, but that my passion for the arts seemed genuine. And in the spring vacation, papa footed all the bills so I could visit her. I played Saint Joan in her "blue room." I sobbed out, "Light your fires . . ." and some of Juliet. I'm sure she said that I showed promise. I went back home, her words still ringing in my ears, "Some day there may be something for you in a play I'll do."

I finished up the college term and started out the summer in a gloomy mood, with fits of restlessness. I cried as though my heart would break while studying Chekhov, feeling close to all three sisters trapped in the provinces. They'd never get to Moscow.

Then came a glorious day when Miss Le Gallienne summoned me. I had not fantasized her words to me. I climbed aboard a train to travel east with pounding heart and boundless expectation. My father made an entry in German in his diary:

June 22, 1937

My daughter Uta goes into the world. Le Gallienne has written her to come to play Ophelia. The little girl took leave this morning. The mother stood beside the train without a sign of what this parting means to her. The train delayed for someone who was coming late. Then Thyra ran beside the moving train. She stopped at the far end of the long platform, like a sailor at the foremost bow of the ship. I saw her from the distance. She looked so small, forlorn and pale. Then it broke out of her, the pain withheld; she wept. It was quite shattering to watch—this mother who was always there, just for her children, till they could fly. Now she has let them go. She comes back home, saws down the birch by Uta's room because it has grown bent for want of light, and hacks the trunk to pieces—as firewood—for winter. It is beginning now.

The family at Sylt, 1922.

With my mother and brother
in Göttingen, 1924.

Contemplating a flower, with my brother, in the garden in Göttingen, 1923.

My brother and I on our first voyage to America, 1925.

Rollerskating in Madison, 1926.

Camping on Lake Michigan with mama and papa, 1928.

Mowing the lawn, 1928.

The Le Gallienne Company, with Miss Le Gee center
(Uta second from right), 1937.

The Sea Gull (Richard Whorf, down left; Uta on platform;
Miss Fontanne seated on right next to Sydney Greenstreet;
Mr. Lunt next to her, back to camera), 1938.

In Ossining, with Letty and
her father, Jose Ferrer, 1941.

With Jose Ferrer in *Angel Street*, 1947.

With Herbert Berghof, 1948.

With Herbert Berghof, 1951.

With Herbert Berghof in *The Lady's Not for Burning*, 1953.

Interior of house at Montauk, 1978.

Mowing the lawn in Montauk, 1980.

The backgarden in Montauk, 1980.

As Charlotte von Stein, Broadway, 1980.

Three generations (Teresa, Letty, and me) on the beach at Montauk, 1981.

Pamela Shandel

The river Leine in Göttingen.

PART III
BETWEEN TWO WORLDS

The East

White clouds of steam blew from the engine of the train and spread a mist across the windows to hide my parents from my view. The train jerked several times, then snorted from the station like a bull. A whistle yowled. A steady clicking of the wheels convinced me I was really underway. The whistle split the air when rounding curves or crossing roads or whizzing through the smaller towns. I was elated by this sound that used to seem so desolate when, in my bed at night, I heard it wail through Madison to leave me far behind.

In imitation of the passengers who nonchalantly sat as though they took such journeys every day, I leaned back by the window, a jaded traveler. Soon I forgot and dropped the mask; I stared intently at the landscape with unself-conscious innocence. The trip we'd taken several times before seemed different now that I was making it alone. I saw the sandstone hills, the scraggly vegetation, the scattered lonely woods and knew that I was leaving them behind. I said goodbye forever to the ugly towns in which I'd played on the forensic team.

I gazed at all the tenements and huts that crowded by the railroad tracks outside Chicago, at rags that waved on clotheslines up above the garbage strewn along the way, at mongrels digging there for scraps. The train slowed down and I could look through windows of the houses. My actor's instincts stirred as I identified with girls who hung about the halls, with families sitting at the tables in their dirty kitchens, a naked lightbulb dangling overhead, a dry geranium on the window sill. I spun out fantasies: if it were me in there, so poor and tattered, how would I play that part?

I buried my anxieties while changing trains on my arrival in Chicago, remembering that my parents had assured me I could manage on my own. With the bravado of a touring star, I found my place on the smooth, streamlined Wolverine Express. I had the whole seat to myself.

Soon we had passed the hideous iron stacks at Gary, Indiana. They jutted up and truly "belched" their filth into the sky. Below, black mounds of coal rose next to sooty hills of sand. I judged man's exploitation of the earth and yet I thought, "This is the world and now I'm part of it." We passed flat fields and plains that seemed to cover all Ohio, without a bump or lump to break the tedium. Each farm or barn seemed miles away from other ones and I felt lonely for the people who must live in them. I wondered at the reason for the endless fences; there was nothing to keep out. I watched a yellow truck and rattling Ford that tried to keep up with the train.

When it grew dark outside, I climbed into my berth, too scared to take off all my clothes. I pulled the blind down just an inch above the window sill so I could still see lights and villages. The wires that were strung like jump ropes from the telephone poles were mesmerizing as they spun along in rhythm to the clicking wheels. But when the train pulled in to towns like Buffalo, the white lights of the station flooded over me and I felt shy. I pulled the shade right down.

At dawn I let the shade up with a snap. I jumped in bed and bumped my head against the upper berth, quite overcome with joy at sights of all the lush green hills that rolled up from the Hudson. This river semed to flow along as lovely as the Rhine. I felt at home.

My brother, who was studying at Columbia University, met me at Pennsylvania Station. For hours, we talked at the same time in our excitement at the brief reunion, and then he put me on a train that travelled to Connecticut.

In Weston, when I'd been there in the spring, I'd seen huge drifts of flowering bulbs beneath the leafless, lacey trees. It looked so different now with summer's foliage. When Miss Le Gallienne greeted me as though we were old friends, my heart was thumping wildly. I was in awe of her. (This never changed.) She took me by the hand and showed me everything. The blazing roses rambled up and over split-rail fences. Off to the right of her white house with sky-blue shutters, was a barn with a real cow, quite pregnant at the time, and hens with chicks that cluckled and squacked and scooted between vegetables or right across the drive. (The calf that came a few weeks later was named Ophelia, which offended me because it was not only innocent but dumb.)

The paths and trails among her woods were lined by columbines and bleeding hearts and clumps of primroses. Wild flowers like the lady slipper, fox glove, trillium were hidden in the underbrush. The birds sang everywhere. Around a bend, a tiny cottage nestled by a hill. It was for guests, or favored actors, in this case. A kennel for the cairns she bred stood in a clearing of the woods. I found it all so beautiful, it seemed to verify my notion that an actor's life was probably ideal.

The actors, like myself, who didn't fit into the cottage stayed at Cobb's Mill Inn, in walking distance. The Inn stood by a pond with overhanging trees, just like a picture postcard. Once it had been a water mill, but now its wheel stood still beside the water spilling down one side of the smooth pond. A mist sprayed out against the fieldstone basement of the Inn. When we ate steaming pasta made by Mrs. Angelini, manager, we could look out across the pond and down the waterfall. I even heard the sound of splashing from my dormer room up on the second floor. It was idyllic.

I felt immediate kinship with the other actors in the company, as though they were another family, and they adopted me, both as a friend and colleague. The play became our life. We worked all day and sometimes evenings, too. I'd make a little progress, then slip back again and often cried because of my comparative inadequacy. But Miss Le Gee (as she'd been dubbed) did not despair and guided every step and breath I took. I gradually believed that I could do it. I also had to rid myself of preconceived ideas of "classic style" that I'd acquired back at the Royal Academy. We didn't just rehearse our parts, we even wove the fabric for the costumes we would wear, on looms out in the barn; and I embroidered mine. It added to the sense that both the role and I were one.

Between the hours of work, I tried out other things I'd never been allowed to do, like staying up all night. I wandered through the woods till dawn and heard wild creatures scurry through the underbrush. I learned that plants and trees put out a sweet, yet acrid smell at night, unlike their daytime scents. I didn't quite believe the owl that hooted every now and then as in a movie. Le Gallienne, wondering why I was so tired when I came to work, decided that I wasn't eating properly.

The end of August, it was time to go to Dennis on Cape Cod, where we would play the play, "I pray you, trippingly on the tongue."

The Cape assaulted me with memories of Sylt. Salt air, the sandy roads with miles of moor and heather on each side, the rolling dunes, all made me sing and talk too much while riding in the back of Miss Le Gallienne's car. I felt immediate affinity for the New England villages, their steepled wooden churches and old salt-box homes, the elms and maples shading the main streets, the scrubby pines behind. A sense of history made me throb now, in the present.

I settled down in a white boarding house and was impressed both by the landlord and his wife and other villagers I met. The sense of privacy, respect for others' individuality was strong among New Englanders, unlike the people in the middle-west.

The theatre stood by clipped hedges and large beds of nicotiana with their furry leaves from which tall, skinny stems emerged topped by the snowy blossoms. They had no smell until the sun went down, but then their scent was almost overwhelming. Each night during the intermission, I plucked a few to use as poor Ophelia's offering in the "mad scene." Perhaps they helped my sense of truth when I was acting, so, when the play received high praise from all the Boston critics, they didn't leave me out.

My family came to share the fruits of my success. They were so proud; but mother spoke as often as she could about artistic discipline, hard work and dedication, of the responsibilities I had to face in this most noble calling. They watched all the remaining performances and, in between, had stimulating talks with Miss Le Gallienne. They whispered when they spoke of me. When I was free, we toured the Cape up to the cliffs of Truro. I fell in love with Provincetown and wondered what it would be like to settle there with some fine painter in a cottage by the wharfs.

In fall, most of the company met once again in Weston to prepare a dozen plays for Miss Le Gallienne's repertory. We were to work for years to ready it. I lived as in a poem at Cobb's Mill Inn. Each day I trudged beside a rushing stream to the rehearsal hall through woods ablaze with autumn colors.

We worked on Chekhov's *Sea Gull*, Ibsen's *When We Dead Awaken*, *As You Like It* and other wonderful plays. We read through them together, worked alone on scenes and brought them in for criticism. She started staging two or three. We even had a fencing master from New York who gave us work-outs twice a week. A voice and speech coach made us toe the mark. At every meal we talked of theatre, as it had been and as it was today. We wrote our journals, learned our lines and listened to good music or some funny anecdotes about what actors had experienced on stage. I missed the piano, so my mother sent me my recorder, on which I played Elizabethan airs that fit Shakespearian plays. And every night I fell asleep to sounds of splashing water.

But then, just like the leaves, my dreams fell, soggy, to the ground and lay in dismal drizzle. Le Gallienne cancelled plans for this particular company, convinced their talents were inadequate for all the difficult plays. Of course, she was quite right, but my heart broke with this first disappointment of my life. I felt quite sure that the last hope for a fine theatre had ended. I hugged her hard and sobbed farewell through rain-splashed windows of the train at Westport.

The crash into the atmosphere of the commercial theatre in New York was quite a shock, but if I really wished to be an actress, I had no other choice. I moved into my brother's "digs" in Greenwich Village. It had three tiny rooms. We washed our dishes in the bathroom sink and used a hotplate for a stove. To us it was a palace.

I was determined to break down the barricades of agents and producers and really wore down all my heels while "pounding pavements." I had my lunch, a ten cent hamburger, at Walgreens on Times Square, together with some other "pros," comparing notes about the casting for the comedies, the melodramas, or the tragedies that were announced as future merchandise. I seldom took a nickle subway or a bus, preferring to save every extra cent my parents had allotted me for this attempt at Broadway, to buy cheap seats for concerts, ballets, plays. Sometimes I even got in free or someone paid for me. These high spots were a substitute for nature which had always fed my soul.

Each time I soared when I was sure I had "the part" and sank to earth when I discovered someone else seemed "righter." However, I felt in the thick of life though I'd been forced to "sacrifice my art for Broadway." I was so young, quite drunk with being an adult.

At last, soon after the New Year, I wangled an audition with the Lunts. Soon afterwards, I wired home, "I'm playing Nina in the *Sea Gull* with the Lunts—on Broadway." I was convinced the whole thing was a fairy tale. My working on the play with Miss Le Gee had obviously helped. I also had no problem of identifying with the stage-struck girl who was drawn back to nature and the lake "just like a sea gull." In spite of this, the next few months were difficult. The atmosphere at the rehearsals frightened me. There was a tension in the air, a nervousness that I had not experienced before. It was as though our lives depended on success. I learned a lot from their excruciating discipline as well as from their fabulous performances, but right up to the end, I struggled to define the actions of my role. Then we "tried out" in Baltimore and Boston and opened in New York. The critics raved. They had "discovered" me. It was a joy as well as a relief. With the éclat of both debuts behind me, I felt I had become a real professional—before one year had passed. However, having worked with masters on two great parts in two great plays, I didn't ask myself, where could I go from here?

Mid-May when the engagement ended, the Lunts set sail for London for a rest. I was to join them in the fall to tour the *Sea Gull* for a while in the United States. In June I went to play in summer stock.

The speed of putting on a play in just a week, when I'd grown used to months of preparation, was almost laughable. But I got used to it. My father wrote me that an artist could make sketches that were meaningful; they didn't always have to be a finished painting. But all the parts I played in summer stock stayed sketches, and each successive one became more frustrating, till after many years, I stopped. However, now, for this first try, I found myself once more in beautiful Connecticut, in Ridgefield.

The Inn at which I stayed was swank with ponds and swans and willows and lush lawns. I played *The Latitude of Love* with a young leading man, so talented, so debonaire that in one week I was in love with him. It was tempestuous. No field, no plot of grass or mossy bank was safe from our embrace. I seemed to be forever looking upward at the sky, at trembling aspen leaves, and all day long, I brushed off twigs and grass from rumpled clothes. We spent the summer in each other's arms off-stage as well as on. I thought that nothing in the world could match this state of bliss. At night the shooting stars fell through the blue-black sky, heat-lightning crackled like my heart.

I had to leave him for two weeks to be with mom and pop awhile before I went on tour. My parents rowed and swam with me on Connor's Lake. We hiked through silent forests. My mother talked of my young man and conflicts that we women had between our love for men and love for art.

One unforgettable day, I rowed with her through the canals that wound out from the lake. The morning sparkled in hot sun, the cooling breezes rustled through the cat tails and the reeds and carried scents of pine. We didn't speak and listened to the dipping of the oars and whirring wings of water fowl. Quietly, my mother began to sing Beethoven's lied "Die Ehre Gottes in der Natur." When at the end, she broke forth like a full-throated lark, the tones rushed upward to the tips of all the pines, and vibrated in air to blend with sounds of nature. The tears poured down my cheeks for joy.

And then I did a dreadful thing. I had my agent send me a telegram demanding I return; it said they needed me at once before the tour. I didn't really mean to shorten time with her, I only wanted to be with my beau a little longer, prior to our separation. I'd barely opened in New Haven when an urgent call bade me to come at once to Madison; my mother was quite ill. I spent a week next to her room there in the hospital. I shouldn't see her, they advised, because she'd realize how serious her condition was. It was a bungled operation.

My mother died. She was just fifty one.

We drove from Madison to Illinois in big black hearses: cremation was illegal in Wisconsin. An Indian summer heat wave made the earth look parched, the trees were almost bare. A road of white cement cut through the barren fields. It shimmered in the heat and a mirage of watery pools loomed between the cracks. I stared, unblinking, at the fields of uncut corn, their dry sheaves rattling death in the hot wind. Though desolation overpowered me, I didn't shed a tear. I couldn't understand. Inside the funeral home, I smelled the sweat of people milling round the ugly wooden box that groaned with heavy, gold chrysanthemums. They shook with sobs when someone spoke in eulogy in quavering tones. To me the words were meaningless. I felt as though I were a robot waiting for the grief I ought to feel. My father was so torn apart he didn't even try to comfort me, and I was much too young to be of help to him. My brother sat in shock.

Back on the tour, I went through all the motions of the play and daily life, but every night I dreamed I saw my mother standing under trees or in a field or by the sea. And when I ran to hold her close, she backed away from me, surrounded by a shimmering light. I called to her and tried explaining that I was the *only* one who knew she wasn't gone. And then I woke and cried. I felt I'd lost my conscience and it didn't matter what I did. That person on whose praise I'd always leaned, whose blame was always justified, was gone and life looked bleak without her.

I came back to Manhattan from the tour and on December 8th in 1938, I married my first love. And we did not live happily ever after.

Our first few years exploded daily like a melodrama. We jockeyed for position every day in conflict over work and play. We fantasized a life where everything was possible. We made our home in Greenwich Village, played on Broadway and in stock and toured pre-Broadway plays. We even took a trip to Hollywood, lured by the studios who offered stardom in great films. They tell me now on the west coast that they are still amazed that we resisted all their promises. It wasn't "art," we said. We didn't like the atmosphere, the values *or* the parts they offered us.

While we were there, I had a strange experience out at Malibu. I almost drowned. I turned my back to a big wave, expecting it to wash across me like the waves on Sylt. It must have knocked me out. All I recall is rolling back and forth in tidal waves beneath the water, eyes wide open, looking all about. I felt suspended, in a blissful state. They say the chemical components of the sea are just the same as in the water of the womb. I must have felt I was back there with mama.

We hied back to New York and played together in *Key Largo* by Maxwell Anderson. When, one fine day, I knew that I was pregnant, it seemed that all our dreams had been attained.

We bought a house on Pinesbridge Road in Ossining, above the Hudson River. It nestled, H-shaped, in a slope of hilly acreage. The fireplace was set against a wall of the long, pine-beamed living room. I put my papa's armoire at one end. It was the only room I can recall where it looked comfortable. A terrace on the opposite side, swept out with flagstones to the lawn, an arbor at the side. Like Ibsen's Nora, I set out to make a nest for both my husband and my coming child. I started scrubbing everything. I rubbed the dowl-pegged floors with butcher's wax until they glowed like gold. I painted flowers on the nursery walls and framed all windows with white organdy, and covered chairs with chintz. Because so much was made by hand, it didn't look conventional. Our acres bloomed with flowers, shrubs and trees that had been planted by the previous owner. I tried to tend them all and mow the lawn as well.

The last few months of waiting for the birth were beautiful. I swung between the periods of serenity in which I knitted five layettes, and those of wildly physical accomplishments inside the house and out. The ninth month came and went and still the baby hadn't come. I thought: perhaps it was so happy in my womb it didn't want to face the world.

The tenth month started drawing to a close. I was on tenter hooks, till in the middle of the night October 14th, 1940, I knew the sac had burst, the water from the womb was running out. With an ungodly spasm in my lower back, the labor started and the fear set in.

Till now I had romanticized the act of birth, the ultimate of nature's miracles. "Labor" was supposed to be hard work, not agony. The terror that ensued grew from my ignorance. My mother was no longer there to help, and "natural childbirth," with the education that accompanies it was unknown. To ease my fear and pain they gave me "twi-light sleep" and other drugs. When doctors and their nurses said to push, "bear down," I thought they were demanding the impossible. Their orders made no sense and seemed designed to torture me, perhaps to kill! The first twelve hours passed in a suspended state of agony; I even wished for death.

They barred my husband from my room the last twelve hours, which made my sense of crisis even more grotesque. Eventually, they wheeled me to a sound-proof "labor room" to shriek and groan in chorus with the other pregnant women, then to "delivery." In this environment, with the strange eyes above white masks, its instruments and forceps and the hands invading all my being, I knew that nature was not just remote but being interfered with. Once when a sound escaped my lips that sounded like the bellow of a dying bull, I was convinced it hadn't come from me, a human female in distress. Just one fleet moment when they put a rosy, slippery infant in my arms and told me it was mine, did I attain that joy I'd dreamed of. But it was gone again when yet another needle sent me to oblivion. It was October 15th, 1 a.m.

I spent another fortnight in the hospital. They wouldn't even let me sit in bed. The joy of nursing was denied because of insufficient milk. They let me hold my child occasionally. I counted all ten toes and fingers, watched her yawn and burp, laughed at her features that looked just like mine and was amazed to learn she was a tiny, perfect, living human being. Her first name stood for happiness, the second for my mother, and so we took Leticia Thyra home to Ossining.

My daughter's first few years were strange for me. The tempo of my life changed drastically. Right at the start, I was fulfilled throughout her waking hours. When she awoke at night and cried for food or needed diapering, I never felt that I was being robbed of sleep. I cared for her with sensuous enjoyment. I shared her pleasure in warm baths, the oiling and the powdering, the sweetness of her flesh, the gurgles and the sudden radiant smiles, abated greed—the sucking motion of her velvet lips, the sun baths on the lawn, the sparkle in her eyes and on her cheeks in brisker weather. With daily satisfaction, I washed linens and her clothes and coddled her in comfort and in beauty.

But all the endless hours that she slept, I wandered restlessly inside the house, around the house outside, and through the countryside. The other occupations I enjoyed had been removed from me. My husband hired a cook who also cleaned, who made me feel that I was butting in or that I criticized if I, too, cleaned or scrubbed or came into the kitchen. The gardner, Sam, came next and when I planted things without his skill, he watched disdainfully. Meanwhile, my husband commuted to New York to be in Broadway plays, acquiring stardom on the way. I thought that mothers should stay home and didn't even look for acting roles. I also knew I couldn't act alone, there in my living room. In search of creativity, I did as I had done in Madison and puttered unsuccessfully with clay or paint, with leather, pewter, brass. I couldn't even drive a car and, all alone out there removed by miles from neighbors and my friends, I wrestled with a sense of emptiness and isolation. What I know now it took me twenty years to realize: I was too immature to give myself to Letty with the same commitment my own mother gave to me. When Letty's needs increased as she grew up, I felt they interfered with mine and got impatient. In my self-centered youth, I must have thought that she was there for me instead of the reverse. I know I damaged her. (When I was very small, I used to think, not just my mother but the world was only there for me and wondered where the others went when I was not around.)

Soon World War II began. Our thoughts were mainly that it meant the end of Hitler. I didn't comprehend the horrors it entailed. I worried that my husband would be drafted, but since we had a child he was deferred right to the end. We did what most civilians did; sent packages abroad, made bundles for the wounded and grew a "victory garden." Each year I canned the fruit and vegetables. Sometimes we gave performances at rallies to raise bonds and entertained the troops back here in the United States.

Until the war, I'd left political involvement to my parents. They both were "liberal." Now I began to shape a point of view through anti-fascism. I got a grasp not just of Hitler but of Franco, of what was going on in Greece and Italy, and started taking stands against the right-wing elements in the United States as well. It was a part of growing up and made me feel I was a full-fledged citizen.

Just prior to the onset of the war, I started acting once again. I felt deep guilt about my parenthood. I played some parts in summer stock and several on Broadway with my husband. We toured a lot and left our daughter in New York with friends and hired help, in nursery school and camp. And in between, at least on holidays, I tried to recreate the atmosphere of the security and love I'd known in Madison. These efforts were a strain and rather superficial.

My husband had "affairs" so I did, too. We thought we were in love with others. Our egos clashed like cacophonic cymbals and lead us to the separation for which we blamed all but ourselves. Just eight years from the time we'd said, "I do!" our marriage lay in shreds. Our daughter was the biggest victim.

I had to prove once more that I could act alone, support myself and now my child. In these things I succeeded.

In spring of 1947, I played in Simonov's *The Whole World Over*. An actor joined the cast when it had opened and, like a storm that cleansed the air and soaked the barren earth, now changed my life. His wide, grey eyes were as mysterious as the sea and, momentarily, he made me innocent again. He took me to the parks where lilac bloomed. He courted me on benches under trees that swarmed with birds and dropped their petals in our laps. All through the nights, he spoke of *art* in acting, not *success*, until we watched the sun come up above the water's edge from bridges or the ferry. We saw the seals cavort up at the zoo and looked at paintings at the Frick. At the Museum of Modern Art, we studied Klee, Picasso and Matisse, then lunched up on the roof. We strolled beside the jostling yachts moored in the Hudson River and took a bus out to the Cloisters or the Botanical Gardens. We picnicked, Renoir-like, on hills in Central Park. My daughter picnicked with us.

He brought back art and nature to my senses; my balance was

restored. My papa loved him, Letty, too, and mama would have loved him even more.

He was a refugee from Austria where he had starred and played with other greats. Here in New York, he acted and directed, too, and taught at his own Studio. He drew me in and forced me to examine my techniques in a new light. I started on the road to "modern" acting. We played in German at the Barbizon with a new company called The Players from Abroad in plays by Goethe, Ibsen, Schnitzler, during which I tested the new things I'd learned. The work was more subjective, not mechanical, the form evolved instead of being predetermined. This was a revelation. For many years I'd felt that acting was no longer challenging. I'd seen the egos soar, that they became enmeshed with outer trivialities. When work was just mechanical, the psyche uninvolved, the needs were for self-satisfaction instead of serving others with one's soul.

With deepening skills and greater understanding of the human beings I portrayed, I won the role of Blanche in *Streetcar* for the national tour and then as the replacement in the Broadway company. I gained new recognition from my peers, not only from the critics. Poor Letty had to go to camp and boarding school.

My liberal stand and my "progressive" actions didn't change although the "hot" war ended and the "cold" set in and nearly froze me to the bone. I felt these pressures moving in on me, as well as all the pressure of my work and pressure on my heart each time my lover was away from me. I needed and demanded his commitment because I felt I'd lost control of my own destiny.

Migrations

My thoughts turned to the past twelve years since I had left Wisconsin. I was exhausted by the drama of my life that had bombarded me on stage and off. I mused, how like the birds we are when our home base seems dry, the climate much too harsh; we want to fly to other shores to seek replenishment. I fled to France.

I noticed little of Toulouse or Carcassonne that passed by windows of my train in the Midi. Occasionally, I thought the view was a Cézanne or a Van Gogh, not actual scenery. My senses were benumbed. Then I arrived in Prades, a village near the Spanish border in the foothills of the craggy Pyrennees. The rocks were red, the gorse was yellow-green. A steepled church stood part way up a hill, but at the center of the town a fat baroque cathedral, seating more than the entire population, dominated. I walked through sandy streets, transported by the strains of Bach that floated from the upper windows of the small stone houses. I heard a flute, a violin, an oboe or a horn that practiced phrases of cantatas. The children in their native dress were whistling Bach, and even skinny dogs sat still to listen, flicking every now and then with their long tails at stinging flies. The dust blown by hot winds lay like a powder on the broad catalpa leaves. Cafés indoors, or those in arbored gardens, were packed with visitors like me who'd come to hear Pablo Casals play Bach, here in this village of his choice. He was a refugee from Franco's Spain. It was a strange conglomerate of art and politics, and the experience was unique for those who came like moths drawn to his flame; the flame that glowed not just for artistry, but with the human statement he had made by silencing his instrument up to this time in protest against fascism.

Back in New York in the mid-forties, I'd become a part of an extraordinary group of people, many of whom have stayed my friends up to this day. For years we gathered regularly at Alexander Schneider's (a founder of the Budapest Quartet, a violinist and conductor). The atmosphere that Sasha, as we called him, had created reminded me of books I'd read about the European salons of the nineteenth century. We ate and drank too much, exchanged ideas and fought for our convictions. Quite often, deadly serious talks turned bawdy and hilarious. Among the notables who came with regularity were: Stravinsky, Milhaud, Balanchine, and Isaac Stern, and Serkin and Istomin, Nabokov, Bernstein and Bil Baird, Gjon Mili with Jane Eakin or Margaret Bourke-White. It was a motley crowd.

Now Sasha had invited me to Prades and lots of them came, too, to listen to Casals or else to play with him. The village throbbed with music and with high ideals. Musicians practiced and recorded all day long, and played their concerts every night at the cathedral. Exhilarated as they surely were by Bach, they went up to their quarters in the mountains every night when the performance ended and played a little Schubert, Mozart, Brahms until the sun came up. Sleep was quite unimportant. Emotions were at such a fevered pitch that tears streamed down, a sweet catharsis: the music was the conduit.

The last performance culminated in all the contradictions of this festival. Those who remained to hear and see were raised to dizzying heights. The dark cathedral with its musty smell of incense was filled to overflow. The oaken doors were left ajar for listeners in the plaza. The people sat so still, the rustling of the leaves outside was audible. Some Spaniards who had crept across the border at great risk, stood flat against the walls like a Greek frieze in bas-relief. In the front row of pews, the Bishop sat in white among an entourage of black-clad priests. There was a feeling of suspense and whispering that none of this should end.

Because applause was not allowed in church, when each concerto or cantata ended, the people simply rose in thanks. Their rising sounded like a flock of birds that flew up all at once. Then there was silence. The clothing rustled as they settled back into the pews. The concert was concluded. When the musicians retired to the vestry, the audience remained in silence in their seats. At last, Casals returned alone, sat down and softly drew the bow across his cello to play "Song of the Birds," a Catalan melody. The church began to vibrate with those tones of deep nostalgia, not just for freedom of the birds but for all people. In front of me a Spaniard fell across the pew with racking sobs; his sounds accompanied the music. The last note faded off. Then, all at once, the Bishop in the front began to clap. The audience gasped before they understood the import of his act. Then they joined in till clapping turned to thunder. This didn't seem enough so we climbed on the wooden pews and stamped like heards of cattle, yelling, "Thanks, Casals," and "Bravo, Pao" till everyone was hoarse. Musicians reappeared to bow and to embrace before the golden altar. And all at once, three girls in Catalanian dress ran down the aisle, a bunch of red carnations in their arms, wrapped in the Loyalist flag. They pushed them at Casals. The audience hushed and wondered what would happen next. He turned his back to us and moved to place the flowers in their leftist flag up on the Catholic altar. The Bishop broke into applause once more, allowing everyone to follow his example. The people laughed and wept, they shouted, kissed and hugged. For just one moment all the conflicts of the world were solved and all oppression ended. I'm still not sure if tears were shed in joy or agony that it was all so simple.

My spirits were refreshed. I left my friends in Prades and went to Nice and Juan-les-Pins. A few dips in the azure sea, befouled by leaking sewage, were quite enough for me and I flew on to Paris. It happened just as I'd been told: I fell in love with the enchanted city.

The light gray buildings were awash with lights and shades of mauve and pink, of lavendar and blue. No tones of yellow were apparent on this unusual palette. Atop the roofs of palaces, museums, office buldings and hotels, the ornate moldings and the statuary conspired with the tiled roofs and rosy chimney pots of smaller houses to draw my eyes up toward the clouds that swept across the Paris sky.

I settled in a tiny room at the Hôtel du Quai Voltaire on the Left Bank. The brass bed with a feather comforter, the grand armoire, the threadbare rug, the porcelain sink, especially the bidet, engulfed me in the worlds of Sand and Zola, Balzac and Colette. Even the cracking plaster walls were a romantic touch. The glass door of my balcony, bedecked with tattered lace, led out onto the Seine. And every morning after waking to the city's bustling sounds, I had café au lait with croissants and fresh jam while looking down at boats and anglers fishing on the Seine, and people browsing at the book and picture stalls along the quai.

One dawn I woke to roaring planes that zoomed like geese in V-formation above the waters of the Seine. The trumpets blared and jet black chargers carrying cavalrymen with glittering helmets thundered down the quais announcing Bastille Day. I danced with workers in the streets and toasted with champagne. I sang the "Marseillese." At night I visited Versailles and watched the fireworks. I ran along the gravel paths or lay on the damp grass to stare while rockets spewed out gold, then showered back to earth like splintered glass. The fountains all alight resembled licking flames. I was a full-fledged Francophile.

My friends were poor, expatriots par excellence who painted, sculpted and composed both literature and music. Jane Eakin and Saul Bellow were among them. Adopting a new role, I fantasized that I was an expatriot, too and shared their lives in ateliers in Montparnasse or high up in Montmartre. I went to their cafés and caves and favorite bistros. I shopped for them, a true Parisienne, at local markets and Les Halles. I chose the new potatoes and the carrots, no bigger than my thumb, the freshest greens and crimson radishes. With wine and fish, a loaf of bread protruding from my arm, some poppies for the table, I was prepared to cook a feast for them on any battered stove. We ate and talked of art while looking out at chimney pots and starry skies. In restaurants I treated them to huîtres, escargots, grénouilles and patés. It was the season for green haricots and fraises des bois. We ate the berries with crême chantilly. No matter where or what we ate, we always smelled of garlic. I sipped Pernod and smoked Gitanes till my head swam, sometimes all through the night. One dawn, while strolling on the quais to watch the rising sun reflect all slivered in the rippling Seine, a rat slid by my feet. I didn't scream, but laughed, "That's Paris!"

Inside the Louvre among pre-Raphaelites, I watched, amazed, while a close friend looked frantically at every single painting. Attempting to discover what they meant to her, she studied them with equal concentration. She had no inkling whether they were done by masters or inferior imitators. It struck me like a thunderbolt how much I owed my papa, how much I'd learned from him, sometimes by sheer osmosis, while being dragged through galleries, cathedrals and chateaux each time we went to Europe.

My pop had made a contract with the University to split sabbaticals in half, to tour in Europe for six months each time three years of teaching had elapsed. He needed new material for his books, and took us all along in 1929 and '32, and then again in '36.

We went to Scandinavia and to Switzerland, the Netherlands and England. Each time we also spent awhile in Germany. I absorbed lots I didn't grasp till later on, of art and architecture, theatre and music in all the different cultures, although my head would often pound and I would drag behind. The landscape I remember vividly.

The trip to Bergen was magnificent. We sailed through fjords past blue-green mountians dancing with the trolls my mother talked about. Peer Gynt and other Ibsen figures came to life in the Norwegian countryside and down in Oslo. While whizzing by Stockholm in motor boats, the city looked like silver in white light. We saw a gloomy drama played outside among real trees and rocks; the actors squacked in Swedish like the sea gulls. I can't forget the day when sitting on a bench with mom beside a pond with swans, I watched a toothless crone who chewed an apple with her gums. Spellbound, I gawked each time her pointed chin collided with her pendant nose. I also learned that it was rude to stare when, with black eyes, she stared right back at me.

The Tivoli in Copenhagen had a rollercoaster far better than the one in Göteborg. I plunged down steep inclines and shrieked with glee and wet my pants in fear.

I thought I might become a nun when walking underneath the mysterious, Gothic arches of cathedrals in Cologne, in Naumburg and in Ulm.

The fort in Würzburg fascinated me almost as much as castles on the Rhine where I had played, when I was even younger, at knights and robbers by a moat and in a real, dank dungeon.

I felt most elegant when strolling down the malls and promenades of old Berlin. The Schwannen Insel and the Grunewald delighted me.

We had a lovely time in Weimar and in Bonn. The homes of Schiller, Goethe, Beethoven, made me believe I'd known them well.

In Munich the huge Pinakotheke quite wore me out, but Mozart's Residenz Theater almost bounced with its Tyrolean baroque décor, and *Figaro* by Beaumarchais was perfect for that stage. The alps seemed like another play. I yodeled on the peaks at Mittenwald, which I preferred to Berchtesgaden. I ran amok in lederhosen and in dirndls, pretending both had always been my native dress. I gasped, then sucked in the sharp air on mountain tops while clouds lay at my feet. The farmers really milked their goats and when I drank the frothy stuff, I thought that

Heidi must have been a living girl and not a figure in a book.

In Antwerp I saw Rubens' nudes, so huge and pink I thought they'd smother me. In Amsterdam we toodled through canals, saw the Vermeers and trembled at the Boschs. I laughed at Breugel, but turned hot and dizzy from Van Gogh's wild, whirling brush.

In London I was more impressed by the white Tower and the Traitor's gate than by the Royal Academy. We'd been to *Murder in the Cathedral* by T.S. Eliot before we went to Canterbury, so when I stood right on the spot where all the knights had slaughtered Becket, I shivered in my boots as though I'd been a witness. When leaving the cathedral gates to have a spot of tea and crumpets, we turned to take a final look: the sandstone church seemd bathed in blood by the reflection of the red setting sun. A judgment of the Lord, I thought.

Now here I stood in Paris, at the Louvre, without my father's guidance and suddenly I knew I was an educated traveler. I had developed personal tastes and knowledge to select, without confusion, the works of art I truly wished to study. Back in my room, I sat on the brass bed to write my father how I felt with love and gratitude. I wrote to him again a few weeks later. I'd made another great discovery.

It was a lovely morning. I wandered out from my hotel across the Pont Royal into the Tuilleries. At the big pond, I watched the children floating matchbox boats or else they paddled with their feet among the quacking ducks. After awhile, I entered the Impressionists' museum. I was quite unprepared for the experience of seeing many paintings of Manet, Lautrec, Degas, Van Gogh, Cézanne, that I had only seen before in reproductions. I stayed till the museum closed and vowed to come back every day. The instant that I left the gallery, I stood stock still; the paintings were *outside*, ahead and all around me. The sunlight filtered through the leaves with the same splotches on the grass, on table tops and on the folds of checkered cloths beneath the striped umbrellas in the Tuilleries, the pond that glittered like a prism in the sun, the silhouettes of children at their games, the gravel paths with daubs of flowerbeds along the edge in geometric shapes, and suddenly I knew: *this* was what art must do, and *to* make us see and feel the world anew.

All summer long such things fell into place. So often during passionate discussions with my fellow artists, I was amazed when problems that they had in painting or in writing were similar to ones I'd recently learned to face when struggling with a role. In our opinion, the creative urge came to a boil when a particular subject was so deeply, personally felt, the artist was compelled to make his statement, his expression. The content must subjectively be wrestled with, its various components separated, honed, and then selectively put into place to make the whole. This was the task. Ideally, the result would have a form; style would *evolve*. The content would communicate to those who saw or heard the finished work. We fervently believed that this procedure was the never ending search for a good artist, precluding smugness or self-satisfaction. Achievement of the ultimate wasn't possible, but struggling for perfection made one's life worthwhile. We felt bad artists always started with a preconception of a form or style which boxed them in; no matter how they tried to stuff it with a little content afterwards, resulting in clichés and imitations, a guarantee of superficiality.

When I go back to Paris now, I run to Sainte Chapelle, that jewel of Gothic architecture in front of Notre Dame. It's almost hidden by some other buildings and many people pass it by, but I go through the doors below and stoop to climb the narrow, winding stairs. Each time I brace myself for the miraculous sight that greets me as I reach the bare stone floor of the 12th century chapel. There are no pews, no statues to detract from all the soaring, stained glass windows that ring the church in place of walls. I stand immovable. The colors are so pure, the shapes between lead frames so exquisite, my spirits are exalted. On days when clouds pass now and then across the sun, the light behind the windows changes; the colors darken, then light up mysteriously as nature plays with art.

At last I felt that I had *lived* in Paris and wasn't just a tourist any more. I got Jane Eakin, my best friend, to come with me to Switzerland and Austria.

We gambled in casinos in Lucerne. (The highest bet allowed was one Swiss franc.) We rode "pedalo" boats around the lake and took funiculars up to the mountains. Chilled to the bone, the mountain peaks obscured by fog, we guzzled wine in a chalet, played cards and talked of lovers that we missed. In Basel we saw many Klees and visited the big cathedral. In Salzburg we saw *Jedermann* in which my lover had once starred. We heard *Fidelio* and saw a beautiful *Twelfth Night*. But, all in all the atmosphere of this particular festival seemed to us commerical, a come-down from the purity at Prades. We left to visit Berthold Viertel at his house in Grundlsee. The village, deep in Steiermark, had a small lake so clear I thought that gods might drink from it. We listened to the poet and director, Berthold, talk with deep conviction of his art and life. He was inspiring. From flower-speckled shores, we watched the native men in Sunday lederhosen climb into boats and row into the center of the lake to blow their Alpen horns. The melancholy notes first hovered in the air, then echoed back from mountain tops.

My lover called from the United States to say he couldn't live without me any more and I winged swiftly back to him.

Tandem Flights

We didn't waste a second when I landed at the airport in New York and flew into each other's arms. My lover was now free to live with me and Letty and, for the nonce, I was ecstatic to be with him round the clock. Right from the start, when he first courted me, he'd won my daughter's heart and she was happy when he joined us now on Washington Square North. And to this day they understand, support and love each other. In intellectual and artistic circles our way of life was quite acceptable but in those days, the "other world" thought it was wrong and that we lived "in sin." Amusing as this seems today, it wasn't easy then, entailing secrecy, pretense, sometimes deceit.

I played Odets' *The Country Girl* on Broadway for a season every night, and in the day resumed my teaching at the Studio. The hours I spent in helping other actors with their work *taught me* more clearly what was wrong with mine.

Next season I played Shaw's *Saint Joan*, the very play that had decided my vocation when I was a child. Jeanne d'Arc was such a force in history, it's little wonder she became the subject for so many writers, painters, sculptors and historians. I probably think that every actress feels a deep affinity for Joan once she has grappled with the character, until she thinks she *is* the little saint. It was the same for me. The times conspired to make it all seem true and in "the trial scene" every night, I felt it was McCarthy, not Cauchon, who judged me and who threatened my beliefs. In any case, my acting deepened through the run. Of course, they didn't really burn me at the stake so my career went on.

For me, the fifties weren't as "fabulous" as many people make them out to be with all their false nostalgia. It was a period of fear, of lethargy pervading people's minds, till even intellectuals became betrayers of their friends, or knelt, obsequious, before the new inquisitors. My lover kept his head and his good sense of humor. He was my strength. The offers for TV and films that used to come with regularity soon ceased. I rationalized that since temptations to gain fame and fortune were now gone, I would stay pure in my attempts to be an artist. It wasn't easy.

Each time I made a compromise to earn some easy money, the Lord would punish me, so when I took a few commercial Broadway plays, they closed in a few weeks, not so "commercial" after all. I played in a "distinguished failure," ruined by bad direction, but otherwise I spent the years pursuing ventures with my love which managed to support our credo and our simple way of life. We couldn't always make producers on the road or in the summer theatres do the plays we really loved, so we did "packages" of Schnitzler, Molnar and Sardou, the lighter fare they felt would suit their audience. A "package" is rehearsed, with all the principal players, more thoroughly than ordinary summer stock, and as it tours the individual theatres supply the smaller roles from their own companies. On several tours we played Fry's *Lady's Not for Burning*, a beautiful play. The parts of Thomas Mendip and his Jennet Jourdemaine seemed made for all we felt and had to say. At other times, my love played Pirandello, I played Eliot. Then, he directed me in Giraudoux and

Montherlant and Ugo Betti. He worked a year on *Waiting for Godot* before directing it on Broadway. I also worked off-Broadway (relatively new in concept at that time), in Brecht and in a play so delicate, so humanly complex, I think it is a masterpiece: Turgenev's *A Month in the Country*.

The only fights we had were with the backers and producers who couldn't understand the plays that we believed in. Then we would do them in "our" Studio and play them for our friends. These battles haven't ended yet. Perhaps we'll live to see the day when serious art will have its day on stage once more and in an atmosphere that's not "show biz" or in "the industry."

The day arrived. My lover made what was to me the ultimate commitment: he said he'd marry me. Ten years had passed since we had met.

Descending through the clouds, we circled high above the mountains of St. Thomas to land at Charlotte Amalie. The smooth Caribbean looked like a quilt in patches of dark blue, transparent jade and emerald green. The demarcations made by deep or shallow ocean beds were sharp, as though a painter's brush had stroked first one bright color, then another, with no attempt to blend the edges. The water was as clear as our intent to marry here.

Our room above the beach was cushioned in hibiscus. The butterflies and humming birds whirred on their golden petals. The trade winds shooed the flies and carried the aroma of the flowering vines. The verdant mountainsides were splashed with bougainvillaea and red poinsettia spiked above damp ferns. The palm fronds rustled, paper-like, while everything that breathed made love: small lizards, like escapees from a pet shop, pursued each other's tails with lightning speed. Excited roosters chased the squacking hens across the street at noon and donkeys brayed their longing from the mountainside at night.

The water lapped our bodies when we floated on the surface, and when we swam below with open eyes, we saw each other, soft and undulating. In Magen's bay we swam among the pelicans that swooped around us catching fish. Through a glass-bottom boat, we watched a world alive with darting fish all colors of the rainbow. They waved their fins and flitted through the coral reefs and timbers of old sunken galleons. We lay together on the silky sand or hunted shells in shapes of tiny breasts or curling genitals. Sometimes it seemed the very leaves were making love when moving in the breeze.

We married in a seventeenth-century fortress that jutted out into the sea. The judge and witnesses were black and white and Scotch and from the Bronx. And when the judge pronounced that we should kiss, our lips met shyly and we looked into each other's eyes with innocence. At that same instant, underneath a window of the fort, a rooster crowed triumphantly. We walked out through the courtyard with our hands entwined for all eternity. A teeming rain had left fat drops aquiver on the greenery. A rainbow arched above the fort and we began to laugh aloud. I knew that we'd been blessed. He was my husband now but always stayed my lover.

Back in New York, there were no new adjustments that we had to make and neither did our daughter. She thought that we'd been married all along. We pitched ourselves back into work and ended up the decade in Vancouver, Canada, playing a Giraudoux. It was a splendid festival.

In 1961, my husband got an offer to be in a film called *Cleopatra*. The site was Italy. Before it ended, our great Roman holiday had spanned the months from late September to mid-May. We made the most of this phenomenal opportunity. Our daughter was away in college and we, worn down by work, made this the grand escape from all our rugged daily disciplines. It also satisfied our dream of visiting Europe arm in arm, and even better than our dream, the visit of a country neither one of us had seen before, so we could share in the discovery. We didn't realize right away the value that the trip would have to feed creative needs. And so we blocked all the concrete realities of present time and place from hyper-sensitive minds and chased euphorically down many paths of Italy's antiquities. We threw ourselves into the roles of pilgrims, tourists, grand gourmets, of archaeologists and art historians. Thanks to the generosity of

20th Century Fox, we lived like kings on the per diem. The salary went straight into the bank (eventually buying a small theatre for our Studio).

We stretched in our luxurious bed and looked through windows of the Grand Hotel at the blue sky of Rome on which the clouds were tumbling, while having our caffe con latte, rolls with marmalade and blood-red oranges. We bathed in the big marble tub and rubbed our bodies with enormous towels in preparation for each day's adventure. There were a lot of them. My husband worked a total of two weeks in the eight months he was on call.

The first few days, we climbed in a carozza and rode behind a dappled horse that wound through all the honking Fiats and the roaring motor bikes. We passed the white and gold clad carabinieri who guard the Quirinal. We travelled different routes with sweeping vistas of the seven hills of Rome, topped by umbrella pines and swirling cypress trees, to me such symbols of this golden city. The stones of Rome glowed with the colors of the spectrum from red to yellow: dark red, burnt orange, rust and terra-cotta, the darkest yellow of the Renaissance, the coral and maroon of ancient brick. The sun stabbed from the gold and copper domes that loomed above palazzi, colonnades and marble churches. We trotted down the cobbled roads along the muddy Tiber. We crossed the bridge between the angel statuary to the fort of bloodied dungeons, Castel Sant Angelo. We drove beside the ruins of Casesar's Forum, past temples and the Roman baths, beneath triumphal arches and the city's gates, through the thick, mossy walls right down the Via Appia.

Of course we didn't always ride. We walked so much we wore down all our shoes. On foot we studied all the monuments. We walked through streets that seemed just like museums, except that people lived in them. I laughed when I saw laundry strung above our heads from sixteenth century palace windows. The ancient churches were in use, not just for tourists; the people prayed in them and had their babies christened there. Sometimes we heard a wedding march or listened to the shuffling feet of funeral processions as we sneaked unobtrusively around to study works of art.

A few steps down below the street behind the Colosseum stands San Clemente, a graceful church with marble floors and pillars. A curved mosaic floats above the altar with some puffy clouds and tiny sheep surrounding Jesus on an open field. This church was built in the eleventh century above a stark basilica that dates six hundred years before. And *this* in turn is built above a pagan Mithras temple where, near the altar, one can see a street with paving stones and gutters for the rain and sewage. In minutes one can climb these stairs and pass through a millenium in which man changed his views and built upon the symbols of his ancestors. The concept staggered us.

We mostly shunned the Hollywood contingent working on the film and other actors whom we knew who thought they were in Rome "out on location." Instead we spent a lot of time with writers and philosophers who'd been my husband's friends in the United States, Italian refugees who, unlike him, had gone back to their country. And they, in turn, acquainted us with others who were native born. Through them we learned to feel the living pulse of Rome, not just the beauty of its outer aspects. They also helped us with our wish to wander from the usual tourists' path toward treasures such as San Clemente.

At times I felt like Alice through the Looking Glass, when tumbling back and forth among the centuries, and with my penchant for assuming roles to fit the time and place, it often came to an identity crisis. Was I a Vestal Virgin or her slave in the old Forum? Was I the emperor's wife who watched the Christians being eaten by the lions in the Colosseum or the martyr in the ring? I could be both. Did I perform on stage at the Teatro right at Marcello's time or was I walking through its ruins with Goethe, or with Browning? How could I go to see the Pantheon with Beatrice Cenci in the morning and play up on a nineteenth century stage with Duse the same night? I fancied Livia's house up in the ruins was mine and when I visited her room, rebuilt in the museum, I viewed the murals with the sky and feathery trees and birds that flew among them with nostalgia for "my" way of life.

When our aesthetic senses reeled, when our heads swam with cherubs, saints and crucifixions, when all the crimes and orgies of the Borgia popes became too graphic for our souls, when early senators seemed indistinguishable from satyrs or the pagan gods, we brushed them from our minds with black espresso and a lemon peel or foaming capuccino. Sometimes we simply took a rest next to the fountains that were splashing everywhere, most often on Bernini nudes.

The food in Rome was sensual; it soothed the soul and soon became almost as much a part of life as studying the art and history. We learned that pasta could be delicate, that making fettucine was an art, that ravioli stuffed with fluffy cheese and spinach was a specialty and that a filleted turkey breast could be a treat. The semolina gnocchi melted on our tongues while we looked towards St. Peter's dome or down at teeming popoli from the café up in the Pincio garden. With Heinrich Böll we settled all the problems of the world while savoring snails around a wooden table at an inn on Via Appia. Together with Max Frisch and Inge Bachmann we lingered between bites of roasted lamb to carry on discussions about modern poetry. We made believe that we "belonged" while eating scampi next to workers in the trattorias of Trastèvere. We chomped on lobsters in the Campo Fiori and ogled Galileo's monument, where he'd been executed. In the Piazza Navona (once the arena for the charioteers) we ate our tortelline at the Tre Scaline and thought of all the lucky stars who had a penthouse there. Sometimes we left the Café Greco after too much Carpano or Strega, and then the Spanish steps decked with chrysanthemums or roses or azaleas (depending on the season) blurred like cascading flames.

On weekends when there was no chance my husband would be called to work, we went into the country. At first we stayed near Rome. We visited the lakes, the papal palace in the Alban hills, and sipped Frascati on the spot, explored castelli and the ruins of Hadrian. We played among the fountains of the Villa D'Este. Once, from a terrace there, I saw a hilltop village in the distance. The more I found that no one knew its name the more I longed to see it. It seemed to have no works of art so it was off the beaten path. Even its road stopped half way up the hill. We parked and climbed on foot past olive groves and donkeys carrying packs. The sandy path turned into cobblestones as we approached "Sabinia." The thoroughfares became steep steps hewn from the rocks. They wound among the primitive houses up the hill. At points along the way, old barefoot women drew their water from the wells into large copper jugs. It was as if we'd climbed into the middle ages. A few young girls wore nylon hose and tight, short skirts, and spike-heeled shoes that made me wonder why they didn't break their legs on the uneven stones. They eyed us with hostility. And suddenly, a radio blared "Volare" in Modugno's voice from windows of a rocky house. It was a paradox. The past and present had collided in a flash that made me know, not only with my head but in my bones, that people stay the same, that only fashion and accoutrements have changed throughout the centuries. (Complexities of human beings in the present are the actor's work, not the perfection of a preconceived historic theatre "style." To make the characters breathe is quite a task, to place them in historic times needs some imagination and less emphasis.) At last we reached the summit of the hill and stood among the ruins of the old fort that once protected villagers from similar invasions.

We felt we were invaders more than once and our Italian friends helped to explain it. The national economy depends so heavily on the "touristi," it makes the people feel, at times, that their whole country is a zoo, their work rooms and their homes are cages, they, themselves, the animals. To stay alive they have to cater to the arrogant whims of foreigners. They swallow pride and cannot snarl in protest. Their national traits are threatened by absorption of so many foreign values. To see the film *La Dolce Vita* on the spot was almost the definitive explanation. We went straight from the cinema to have some coffee on the Via Venetto. There, life seemed still more decadent than that reflected through Fellini's eyes.

In Rome, the Villa Giulia housed Etruscan art. The humor that revealed itself in pots adorned by faces peering in to see what might be cooking there, the twinkling smiles on effigies on top of tombs and coffins, the box lids with their handles shaped by dancing couples, were all so witty and sophisticated, it was impossible to think they'd been conceived almost three thousand years before. We chased Etruscan culture up the coast with visits to the Cerveteri and then Tarquinia, exploring all the excavated streets and tombs that glowed with colors of the snorting bulls and nudes and plants, the symbols of ferility that decorated even death.

We spent a balmy day at Ostia Antica, the ancient port of Rome. We even brought a picnic lunch of bread and cheese and wine like Romans did. We walked through grassy streets among the gently crumbling ruins. Unlike Pompeii where one can see the terror of a people struck down while caught in daily action, we felt that here the families had moved away in peace in search of fresher fields. Some walls of faded brick remained and we went in and out of buildings like old residents. We played both audience and actor for each other in the shell of an arena theatre. Our sole companions were the grazing sheep who stopped to gaze with questioning frowns. We wandered further in the ruins and found a toilet with an out-house seat, but made of marble. A kitchen floor made of mozaic tiles was splashed amusingly with pictures of fish skeletons and carcasses of fowl, as though the cook had dropped the garbage on the floor. I don't know why no decorator has copied this.

We went by train to Florence with just three days to take it in, and worked ourselves into a feverish state by thinking of the things we'd miss or never see again. We knew that an entire year would not suffice to *really* see so many treasures of the Renaissance. If there'd been time, I would have spent an hour with each Donatello and Verrocchio. I would have lived in Fra Angelico's painted cells and prayed in Giotto's chapels. I would have stayed a week in the most perfect little church in Italy, San Miniato al Monte. I would have made myself a guide for the Bargello, a nun to walk for years through all the lovely cloisters.
We stood in silence in the church of San Lorenzo and suddenly an organist began to practice Bach. My husband took me in his arms when I began to sob at such a perfect moment. Not just the Duomo pushing upward toward the sky made our

hearts thump, but all the white and yellow campaniles with countless delicate arches. And when their bells tolled through the town at vespers or at matins, we were transfixed in time.

My husband had to leave to work in Rome while I stayed on in Florence for another week. I spent each night devouring books about the ruling Medicis and all the artists they had fought among themselves to patronize. All day I ran just like a greedy child to gulp up works I'd fleshed out by the reading. I was awhirr with images of marble: jet black, dark brown, a sandy-orange, palest yellow, and shades from red to pink to purest white. What artistry it took just to *select* from marble quarries for facades and walls and floors, for statues, columns and the fountains. I wondered, mystically, if God had pointed to this spot in Tuscany, this valley by the Arno in the hills of Florence, Fiesole, Siena and San Gemignano, and picked his men to use like powerful, creative funnels through which to sift the elements of air and earth, the light, the rocks and pigments, to make great art at one with nature?

We erred again and tried to see the whole of Naples, Capri and Pompeii in just one weekend. It was hysterical. We grated on each other's nerves and argued over things we ought to see, mozaics that we'd passed, the theatre ruins our guide had missed while showing us the ancient brothels and the plumbing. We tried to put our blinders on in order *not* to see the devastating poverty, to keep our eyes instead on things like cloisters paved with bright majolica, so yellow that we thought the sun had just come out above the lowering sky. At the Museo Nazionale, the span of centuries dissolved again when I ran toward Pompeiian paintings dated 49 B.C. and thought they were Picasso, 1949 A.D. We wasted time at a performance of *Don Carlos* that would have been laughed at on Bleecker Street. Although the Neapolitan opera house was a real masterpiece, we might have viewed it in the day for fifty cents.

We zoomed to Capri on a hover-craft that didn't touch the water of the famous bay. I thought it was symbolic. In retrospect it was a lovely day: December, cold and grey, no other tourists were in sight. I still felt mad Tiberius brooding on this lonely rock. We had our fill of San Michele, then lay down on our backs in the small boat to beat the tide into the blue, blue Grotto. The oarsman really sang "O Sole Mio." Because we had so little time we settled for a guide who drove for many miles, then stopped to point with pride: "Ecco! la casa di Ginger Rogers!"

If I could choose a day in which to live again it would be one we spent with Saint Francesco in Assisi. It was mid April. We set out from Rome in the compartment of a train that passed so slowly through the mountain towns of Umbria that we could lean out of the window, barely ruffled by the wind. We smelled the almond blossoms and the oleander trees. Wisteria hung from mountainsides and buttercups were glistening in the fields.

Our first stop was Perugia. From its high ramparts we could see Assisi rising from a nearby hill. How strange to think these neighboring villages warred throughout the middle ages. We visited the Duomo and Palazzo dei Priori, saw carvings in the Cambio and fell in love again with paintings of Massaccio and the native Perugino. At dusk we got aboard the train and wondered if we hadn't erred to take our leave so quickly. The night was dark when we drove through Assisi's massive gate. The streets were dimly lit and the stone houses pressed so close, they seemed to smother us. But, from the instant that we entered the Subasio Hotel until we left the village the next night, we thought that we'd been touched by magic. Our room, in the hotel carved from the rock, had a brass bed and pale blue walls, white curtains and a little chandelier suspended from the ceiling. A vase was filled with freesia. We curled up in the bed.

My husband nudged me out of sleep in order not to miss the Umbrian dawn. He'd pulled the curtains back so we could look out at a Renaissance masterpiece. A few bright flowers bloomed in splashes on the valley's red-brown earth. I learned what "umber" really meant. In tidy rows, pruned Judas trees stood starkly with their branches reaching up in gnarled supplication. The distant hills rolled up to the horizon in a blurred bluish-green. The church bells in the valley and Assisi tolled out for Sunday's services, and on the terrace just below our room we went on drinking in the view together with our coffee.

We whispered as we started on our pilgrimage to follow in St. Francis's steps. At first we thought it was a mystic sign that birds and doves were singing, cooing everywhere, that donkeys trod so lightly, until we realized that this hill had been a wild life sanctuary for so long that even rabbits weren't afraid.

We went to the Basilica adorned by many Giottos. We marveled at the church itself and at the works of all the geniuses who'd offered up their labor to the gentle Saint. His sense of brotherhood, renunciation of his wealth, resistance to corruption of the church was still reflected everywhere. The crypt with his remains was awesome in the flickering candlelight. Symbolically, we lit a candle too and stood awhile in silence.

We went to see where San Francesco lived and played and where he'd serenaded Chiara, and later, where he'd asked her, too, to take the vows. We drove up to the mountain's top and visited the hermitage and when I saw the tiny pillow he had carved of stone to rest his head, I almost wept. All day men's actions seemed to spring from love, so when our driver ran to pick a bunch of cyclamen for me, I took them gratefully, without surprise. Before we left, we went the second time that day to Santa Maria Maggiore, to meditate within the pristine atmosphere of this fourth-century church. We left inspirited. Saint Francis put us in a state of grace.

My husband's "work" was finally done. We really threw our coins into the Trevi fountain with fervent hopes that someday we'd return.

Back in the U.S.A. our work resumed with vengeance. All summer long we taught and got the Studio back in shape. Then I began my stint in *Who's Afraid of Virginia Woolf* and he played *Andersonville Trial.* I can't think how our trip had tangibly helped to mold our roles. I *do* believe that our creative juices flowed at peak from our well-nourished souls.

In winter 1963, I flew to London with *Virginia Woolf.* My daughter was already there attending drama school. Now that she was an adult our feelings changed. We formed a lasting, grown-up friendship. The times I suffered more than usual from the cold, the rain, the snow and sleet, when absence from my husband seemed unbearable, she comforted and gave advice that always helped. She shared her favorite haunts with me and I, in turn retraced my many steps of 1937 just for her. It wasn't only weather that oppressed me so; I was exhausted by my role and made more desperate by the lengthy separation from my husband. When I returned, I actually started sobbing at the airport and didn't stop till I arrived at home: the sky was *blue*. I hadn't seen that since I'd left.

It fascinated me to learn how different London seemed to me when I returned together with my husband in mid-December in the seventies. (The trip was paid for by my small part in a "horror" film.) When we held hands it didn't pour but seemed a gentle rain. We didn't think of fog; it was a hazy mist that cast a spell on all the lovely parks with duck-filled ponds and tiny gulls and graceful bridges. The riders trotted down the lanes straight from a Constable canvas. In Kensington the ghost of young Victoria danced. And when it snowed, the flakes fell cheerfully around the heads of carollers who sang before St. Martin's-in-the-Fields. Trafalgar Square was festive with the countless pigeons and a giant Christmas tree. The changing Guard at Whitehall and the Palace made us laugh when they maintained the strictest etiquette through sloshing sleet. We stood enthralled back in the Poet's Corner of the Abbey during choir practice. We walked along the Strand and through Wren's finest churches, then rested in Dickensian pubs. The beech trees on the Tower grounds were shedding bark as if an artist had peeled off the spots to match the ancient walls. We went to plays and sumptuous restaurants. And the last day, we watched a Turner sun set on the Thames. When parliament, Big Ben and Whitehall glowed with festive lights, my husband put his arm through mine and we both wondered why I hadn't always known it was a splendid city.

With money from the "horror" film, we flew on to Vienna, the birthplace of my husband, the city which still echoed

Haydn, Mozart, Schubert, Strauss, the city which reflected Schnitzler, Nestroy, Rilke, Hoffmansthal, and in my husband's mind, his father's socialism, the writings of Karl Kraus, the theatre of Reinhardt, Kainz and Moissi. It was our second visit there together.

The first, in autumn 1969, had lasted just a week in which not just my husband but the city seemed to woo me with its charm and elegance. Champagne corks popped at once, a violinist in a red, gold, crystal dining room played waltzes while we sipped our soup and sampled Tafelspitz.

We trotted round the city of the inner Ring in a fiacre before exploring it on foot. Important sights were all approachable, not overwhelmingly spread out the way they were in Rome. After a mass at the St. Stephan's Dom, we climbed the endless stairway to its golden roof and looked down on the lovely town. Together we retraced my husband's steps to his academies and former homes. Sometimes he paled and I stood by in silence when painful memories swept over him. He treated me to coffee in his favorite haunts and took me to the taverns where, while eating Würstel with his colleagues, he'd planned to change the theatre, perhaps the world. Today, a lot of those same colleagues are still struggling with Hitler: who was a Nazi, who was not, intrudes on endless conversations. A sense of guilt pervades.

The balmy weather lured us to the Prater and the Wienerwald. We picnicked on the Karlsberg and saw the Danube in the distance winding brown, not blue. We drank new wine at Heurigen in vineyards out at Nussberg while the October sun streamed down on us.

The last of all the Hapsburg Empresses, Elizabeth, or "Sissy" to her subjects, had always fascinated me. She came alive in all the salons and the ballrooms of Schönbrunn, the Hofburg, and at Belvedere. She was incredibly slim and beautiful, but when I saw her gymnasts's bars and rings all fastened to a gilded wall above the smooth parquet, her mystery was dispelled. I howled with laughter.

My recollections of the second trip spin through my head just like the snow that flurried through Vienna's streets. With flam-

ing cheeks and breath that puffed in clouds, we joined the
Christmas shoppers in the Kärtnerstrasse. The churches filled
with candlelight and worshippers and hummed with song and
services from dawn till late at night. At stalls of open Christmas
markets we bought some ornaments and wreaths to add a festive touch to our small room at Hotel Sacher. It was unneces-
sary since it already had red damask walls and drapes, a crystal
chandelier, a curtained alcove for the feathered bed that stood
below a painting of two naked cherubim. It also had a balcony
that overlooked the decorated streets. We thought perhaps we
should begin rehearsing Schnitzler's *Anatole*. On Christmas
night we heard *Der Rosenkavalier*, on New Year's eve, *Die Fleder-
maus*. And in the Hofburg chapel all the heavens parted when
the Sängerknaben sang a Mozart mass. And yet I sensed that,
like so many Viennese, I clung to memories of the past though,
unlike them, I didn't need reflections of old Hapsburg glories. I
finally knew that I lived *now* and for tomorrow.

We flew back to New York, our senses sated, prepared to work
and work and work. I realized I was leaving happily, without re-
gret, that Europe was for visiting, America was where I lived. It
was my home.

A Home to Roost

The rain was pounding on the canvas top of the convertible and whipping through the leaky windows. Though windshield wipers beat the water back and forth, the road was hard to see. White lightning sizzled through the sky and thunder roared like cannon. We pulled off to the side until the storm was over. Almost as quickly as it had begun, the rain came to an end, the heavy clouds were gone. We buttoned back the canvas top and by the time we climbed back in the car, the sun was beating down.

We had escaped the hot and dirty city, not just the storm. The boring highway narrowed to two lanes and soon we came around a bend. There seemed to be a bank of snow. We stopped the car again and read the sign: Long Island Ducks. They snuggled close and looked like fluffy snowballs. Some squacked or preened themselves while others waddled to a swampy river bed to cool themselves. No earth was visible because their feathers

125

covered everything like a white carpet.

We were enroute to see the lighthouse at the tip of the South Fork. We drove past huge potato fields and acres of blue cabbage and, now and then, through fields of corn and yellow wheat. With windmills etched against the sky, I wondered if I wasn't in the Netherlands.

We walked around East Hampton's pond, reflecting green from maples, chestnuts and the weeping willow trees. We looked at headstones in the cemetery, some dated 1632. We saw the saltbox houses, rambling inns and clapboard 19th century homes. It is reputedly the prettiest village in America. That may be absolutely true.

We'd just passed Amagansett when the landscape changed as suddenly as the storm. Gone were New England streets, the rolling lawns and steepled churches. Instead, below us stretched a vast expanse of moor and dunes that heaved down to the sea. Scrub oak, beach plum and bayberry shrubs clung to the sand in clumps between the gnarled black pines. A smell of salt and heather and warm pine pervaded. Tears stung my eyes. Was it a trick, this strange mirage of Sylt? My childhood rushed at me.

We climbed a hill from which we viewed the boundless sea and mused that Portugal was next, beyond the blue horizon. We drove through oak and hickory woods. A deer and doe looked back at us, completely motionless. A family of racoons went rambling by the road. We drove right through the town of Montauk till we reached the Point where once there'd been a fort and Washington had kept the British ships at bay. We climbed the cliffs, rolled down the dunes, splashed in the surf and looked off at Block Island. While driving back, straight at the orange sun, I made a secret vow that someday I would settle there, no matter how my life might change or what I'd have to do to earn it.

We came again for many years whenever we could manage and spent our weekends in motels or borrowed cottages. When that seemed not enough, we rented houses by the month. We started thinking Montauk was "our town." We fantasized that houses being built were really ours and looked at all the ones that said "For Sale." We were especially drawn to the Erosion

Cliffs that lay beyond the town. They soon became our habitat. We walked past lily ponds and through the reeds and cattails looking for wild mint and other seashore plants. The rabbits scurried at our feet and sometimes, accidentally, we flushed a quail. Atop the highest cliff we looked down eighty feet at boulders scattered on the soft, white sand below, at surf that rolled up on the beach and out to sea at yachts that trawled for fish. My husband speculated, "Who needs Capri?"

In 1962 just after Labor Day, my husband went to fill the car with gas for our return to New York City. I lied and said I had to say "goodbye" to our good friends who dealt in real estate. Instead, I said "hello" and put down money for a piece of land adjoining the wild cliffs. My friends said, "Hurry up! Your Beetle doesn't hold much gas," and then I signed a deed of ownership. I waited till there was no turning back, until the builders started breaking ground to tell my husband that at last we had our earthly paradise. He was elated, adding that we had to build a birdhouse, too.

For months we argued with the architect. Our spirits rose and fell as though we had a fever. One day we thought that everything was going well, the next, each door and window sill seemed wrong. The door knobs and the buttons on the cabinets were the last straw. In June we finally moved inside and drank champagne to christen it the Rooster, because it roosted on the hill that overlooked the sea and seemed to crow just like the one that had announced our wedding.

Like a young bride in her first home instead of a wise matron in her last one, I scrubbed and waxed until my husband warned, "You'll rub this little house to death." I painted roosters on the kitchen walls and flowers in the bathrooms. My husband begged, "Hands off!"

The rooms and all the furnishings were placed to lead the sight out toward the sea and landscape. The windows reached from floor to ceiling. I polished them so not a smudge would blur the ever-changing panorama.

My wonder at the movement of the sun remains with me. In

spring, a streak of light appears above the moors. The sky is dark. At times a few stars are still visible. The light spreads slowly upward turning pink and orange. And suddenly a sliver of hot light peeks over the horizon. Within a count of ten, the flaming ball has risen up and hangs suspended for a moment before it climbs on high. In case the ball is truly red, I take the warning like good sailors do; a storm is brewing. When clouds are hovering in the sky to shroud the sun for a few moments, the rays behind them streak out radially and I have visions of a Tiepolo or Titian painting. In autumn, when the orbit of the sun has changed, it rises over water and when it's very cold, the sea is bleached, so pale it seems much lighter than the sky at the horizon. Then, as the sun comes up, its shimmering reflections on the ocean are pastel.

Along the coast, the setting sun plays other games. In fall, it sets above the water, in early spring, almost behind our house. I love it when it seems to set the lamb-like clouds ablaze and skies behind turn garish, bluish-green. Then pines and Russian olive trees, the roosting gulls and starlings on the wires appear in silhouette. We stand in silence till the flames die out, the sandy cliffs turn bloody red and undersides of breakers on the shore turn pink. The colors fade to mauve and it is twilight.

Indoors we light another blaze in the brick fireplace. We sit close by the crackling flames and leave a window open so that the whiffs from driftwood and the cedar logs escaping through the flue can waft back in the house. The only light comes from the fireplace until the moonlight casts a silver path on the black water. Each night we fall asleep to sounds of pounding waves. And now I know familiarity breeds ever growing wonder, certainly no contempt.

I stood in awe of my responsibility for land on which no one had lived, no spot of which was ever cultivated. The native growth was ragged in the spring before it greened. Wild cherry, shad and summac trees were twisted by the winter's wind. The clumps of blueberry and bayberry shrubs, each needed room to breathe. From May till Fall, I was surprised by all the things that popped up in between the tufts of goose grass and the reeds:

wild violets and strawberries, white daisies, black-eyed susan, rambling roses, partridge-peas and dusty Miller, clover, dandelions, Pye weed and goldenrod, wild asters, ferns and bachelor buttons, all trying to survive the onslaught of the honey-suckle and the worst of all the smotherers, the deadly nightshade, bittersweet and blackberry vines.

The first few years I let God have his way and concentrated on the dirt piled up by builders all around the house. With help from a fine landscape artist and his men, I terraced the steep incline in the back and decorated it with marble chips, some hollies and a flaming barberry bush. They laid broad steps of railroad ties from the front door up to the bedroom deck and finished walks around the house with flagstones. Protecting flower-beds and future plantings from the winds, we set out junipers and pines—Japonicus—with needles that explode like fireworks and grow almost a foot each year.

When taking cuttings from euonymus and planting them beside the house, I waited breathlessly for them to grow right up the walls. The nurseryman said, "In ten years . . ." and he was right. The ivy was the same. Climbing hydrangea, on the other hand, grew fast and quickly framed the kitchen window on the second floor with pendant blooms. Two slips of star-shaped clematis that blooms in mid-September reached the upper deck in just four years and now adorns it with sweet smelling, ivory flowers.

Somehow I got it in my head that mowing lawns was middle-class. I pitied all the fools who were "enslaved" by gardening. My answer was to plant a care-free "meadow-mix" which, I was told, included grasses, clover and wild flowers. I never saw a single flower, just dandelions and ugly grass that grew so tall it buried all the shrubs and flower beds from view. Within a month I mowed and started yanking out the rankest weeds, replacing them throughout the years with fescues and Kentucky blue. Now it's a carpet underfoot and sets off all the plants like lovely paintings. Each year I pushed back further into virgin growth and dug out rocks and rope-like roots, the thistles and the nasty underbrush. I added compost and manure until the earth was friable and ready for all vegetables and flowers. If this is "slavery," give me more of it. My callouses are my badge of honor.

It took me years to learn that, by the sea, the salt air and the strong prevailing winds would not allow a re-creation of my childhood garden. The saplings of white birch and mountain ash, the fruit trees and the peonies I hoped for, died when flailing winds that carried salt would burn them black or knock them down. Soon after that, I followed nature's suit so near the sea with Russian olive trees, crabapple, ilex, cedar trees, azaleas, rhododendron in all shades, and many lilac bushes. The season's early bulbs have multiplied until the spring brings many drifts. The shad and cherry trees that bloom so white out on the moors are echoed on our land.

The tulips and blue hyacinth are often victims of the rabbits and the deer. These creatures I once loved, near whom I spoke in whispers or admired from afar, are now my mortal enemies. I'm sure they passed around the word that at the dead end of the road next to the cliffs, a lady lives who grows delicious food for all the animals, including lettuce leaves and bushy carrot tops. They came with families, then in herds to visit, nibble and destroy. Deterents stopped their work as soon as all the deer got used to even the most noxious ones. My arsenal of rocks diminished as I pelted them. In any case, my aim was bad and then the deer would turn to smile derisively. My stomping feet and clapping hands, my shrieks, "For shame, for shame!" amused them even more. In desperation I erected stockade fences and meshed wires at the vulnerable spots so nowadays they only come bi-annually to walk straight down the terrace steps for a fast, deadly forage.

The rose in hundreds of varieties is surely a phenomenon. I love the texture and perfume of cultivated ones, and seafoam roses, aptly named, that ramble near the ground. I'm glad I added blaze to the split rails up on the hill. But, most of all, I cherish the rugosa rose which is so common by the sea that many people barely notice it. I love it not because it's indestructible, not just because of its sweet scent or tones of modulated pink, but just because it tumbles like the children on the beach, ungroomed and windblown. It blooms throughout the summer, and in Fall, instead of pinching off dead flower heads, I let them go to seed to form "rose hips." Between the leaves they look like Tiny Tim tomatoes and bring both cheer and nourishment. I use them to make jelly and a wine that tastes like good Tokay. The rose hip brings to mind Fry's lines when Thomas woos his Jennet in *The Lady's Not for Burning*:

> . . . I can pass to you
> Generations of roses in this wrinkled berry.
> There: now you hold in your hand a race
> Of summer gardens, it lies under centuries
> Of petals. What is not, you have in your palm.
> Rest in the riddle, rest; why not? . . .

Nippon daisies, known on Long Island as the Montauk daisies, grow all around our house. Most of the year you'd think they were a dark green bush distinctive only for their pungent, almost sexy smelling leaves. But when chrysanthemums and dahlias bloom in orange, rust and yellow, like a carnival, when marigolds have reached their peak, the Montauk daisies open up white blooms as large as saucers and their centers are like yellow powder puffs.

My horticultural talents developed through the years with help from growing compost heaps. When asked which is my favorite vegetable or herb or flower, I always say, it's like the parts I play, the one I'm working on must be the best. I really love them all, each year anew as though I'd just discovered them, like the four seasons.

We take our lessons from Thoreau and tread the ground so softly that the pheasants and the quail are undisturbed while we are harvesting the fruit and berries on the moors and in the bogs. Through local friends we found the spots where vines and bushes bear abundantly. We guard them zealously because the casual visitor so often strips them clean with little knowledge of their ripeness or their future care. They trample them and strip the fruit, then toss it in a ditch when, as with beach plums, they find out they have to cook them first. When our own harvest is complete, we pause to listen to the droning bees and look across the fields that shimmer in a haze so like a Wyeth or Jane Eakin. Sea lavendar blooms at summer's end and blows like Belgian lace. We wade across the salt marsh, picking it by armfuls for ourselves and for our friends. At Christmas time we go to hills beside the bay and choose the hollies with the reddest berries. We pick them with great care and cursed when ignorant marauders hack away so ruthlessly.

The bustling life around the docks and the marinas with their boats and flags and swooping gulls and flapping fish has always tempted painters. Each week when I go for supplies, I brace myself against the salty spray and cast my eye on all the Winslow Homers and wish I, too, could put it all on canvas.

Not just the Tumas, Gossmans and the Duryeas, but other fishermen can trace their ancestors back several hundred years to times when Montauk Indians hunted and went fishing there. Each year the "blessing of the fleet" makes clear the rough life for the men at sea who keep themselves and all of us well fed. A priest waits on the dock, the nuns stand by, the acolytes swing incense and the people cheer as boats float past, bedecked with colored flags and streamers. A hush descends when, all at once, a boat appears completely draped in black; a man has died at sea.

While waiting for the latest catch, we sit on stools next to the clam bar guzzling beer. We watch the loaded boats chug into port. If people spoke in other languages, you'd swear you were in southern France or Portugal.

Below our house, down on the shore, sandpipers flit on matchstick legs and race the tide to catch the insects. Sea ducks ride back and forth on rolling waves and wait to bob their heads into a school of fish. The gulls line up like soldiers on the cliff behind us to wait for prey or a free ride on currents of the air. At times the beach is smooth or lies in rippling drifts completely free of stones. After a storm, the sand erupts with rocks and endless pebbles. I was so dumb, for years I thought the waves had washed them up on shore. Not till I found a marble rock I hadn't seen for months, back in the self-same spot, did I begin to understand: it wasn't rocks that moved but *sand* that washed away and then washed over them again. Except for litter left by careless campers, there's little on the beach we don't appreciate: the rubbery weeds that look just like Medusa's hair and the black pods that lie on shore like tiny pre-historic creatures, and skeletons of fish reminding one of modern art. I gather crabs and mussels, save the opaline shells and use the stones for my rock garden. The seaweed makes a perfect mulch and fertilizer, the driftwood is décor or firewood. Of course we swim and surf bathe when it's hot and let the breezes dry us off.

We got the birdhouse that my husband sought and now I can't imagine life without the purple and the yellow finch, the kinglets, cardinals and flickers, the spotted sparrows and the cooing morning doves, or Jimmy Cagney, my impertinent chicadee. The latter actually follows me around the garden when I do my chores. He perches on a branch and chats and yells as though he were advising me. I don't know which is funniest; when birds get mad and throw their seeds about for spite, or when they hop into their bath, take a long sip, throw back their heads to let the water trickle down their throats, or when they splatter on their underbellies in the bath and sound like little whirring engines.

When I'm away, I worry that they'll miss their daily feed and that the smaller ones will not defend themselves from all the grackles and ferocious jays I usually shoo away. But then, when I return, they're there to greet me, waiting only till I fill the feeder to resume their merry antics.

The birds are like the land on which I live: I do a lot for them (although I know that they could do without me), they do much more for me. I know that I must guard the things that bring me so much sustenance. I must protest to those who ruthlessly exploit, neglect, abuse the land, the sea and air, those people who don't hesitate to foul the nest, this earth of ours.

Sometimes, while soil is crumbling softly in my hands, when working all alone outdoors, I'm suddenly arrested by a flash involving all my senses. I am suspended by the solo warble of a finch, a taste of salt air on my tongue, my nostrils flare with scents of pine and new-mown grass, a breeze licks gently by my cheek and a strange aura looms around a single plant or tree. My tears well up spontaneously; I let them flow in ecstacy. But then a gull emits a comic wail, my dogs run up with wagging tails; I laugh. The spell is broken.

At such a time, I often think about the people who take drugs to reach euphoria, or those who need a tranquilizer to find peace, not knowing they are really dulling all their senses. I think with pity of the people who join cults to fill a vacuum in their lives, believing that will be their answer, ignoring all the inner strength, the spurts for their creative energy which they can find in nature.

My real vocation isn't farming, managing a house or cooking for my friends and family, but all these things are truly recreation, a re-creation of my urge to be an artist. The roots that I've put down in Montauk serve me well. Out here I've worked on many roles, have written books and made translations of some German plays. The last one was *Charlotte*, a play by Peter Hacks, in which I played the only character. I even managed to persuade my husband to conduct a few rehearsals here and raced around our living room with vistas of the ocean for a backdrop. I played the part on Broadway and then, joyfully, on tour for several years. With every fiber of my being I want to act, and act until I die. I hope that I have learned to be a better artist, that I'll keep on growing. With all that has been given me, I want to give it back, because the ultimate is not fulfillment of oneself but being of good service to one's fellow man.

Afterword

Teresa, now I've told you almost everything. I have omitted only the disasters of my life which many others love to revel in; the hurricanes and floods, the fire, the nearly fatal crash, the many illnesses I faced and overcame, miscarriages that almost broke my heart and, worst of all, the deaths of many friends. Since I believe that cynicism is akin to madness, I'm not ashamed of the exuberance and innocence with which I view my life. I side with Thornton Wilder in *Our Town* when he reveals how sad it is to let our daily joys pass by while they are happening, only to know in *retrospect* how beautiful they were.

Sometimes I wonder if my mother knows what she has given me. At least I'm very glad I've passed it on to you.